I CHOOSE LOVE

FRANK CAPRI

Copyright © 2021 by Frank Capri

All rights reserved. No part of this book may be reproduced or transmitted in any form or by any means, electronic or mechanical, including photocopying, recording, or by any information storage and retrieval system, without permission in writing from the copyright owner.
This work is based on the experiences of an individual. Every effort has been made to ensure the accuracy of the content.

I Choose Love

This book will change your life. Guaranteed.

Author: Frank Capri

Editor: Judy Louise

Layout: Michael Nicloy

ISBN-13: 978-1-957351-04-9

Published by
Nico 11 Publishing & Design
Mukwonago, Wisconsin
www.nico11publishing.com

Be well read.

Quantity orders may be placed with the publisher via email:
mike@nico11publishing.com

Printed in The United States of America

CONTENTS

Prologue	13
BOOK 1	**15**
God's Way	19
My Peaceful Work	20
With a New Day	26
What's the Meaning of Life?	28
Resentments	30
Fear Driven	31
Money (Greed)	33
Approval	34
BOOK 2	**41**
Worry	45
Keep it Simple Stupid	47
You Had It All Along	49
Cause and Effect	50
Head Trip	51
Deception	52
Watch What You Ask For, You Just Might Get It	54
From the Beginning	57
Weakness	58
Agape Love	60
The Force of Love	67
The Goal is Agape Love	69
He Died For Me	71

Book 3 — 73

We're All Special, Even Though — 75
Special – Valuable – Precious and LOVED — 77
Co-Dependence as a Good Thing — 80
The Love of God! — 82
External Farts in Our Head — 83
Been There, Done That — 86
Internal vs. External Motivation — 87
Opening a Can of Worms — 88
God's Pipeline — 91

BOOK 4 — 99

Keep Doing What You Always Did -
        You'll Get What You Always Got — 100
Love God Back! — 108
Have Faith, Trust More, and Stop Complaining — 111
Life is All About It — 115
Shouldn't Life Be to Just Love? — 117

BOOK 5 — 121

Our Insides Cannot Change — 122
A Very Common Denominator — 125
God Didn't Gamble on You or Me — 128
Self-Will — 131
We Keep It by Giving it Away — 133

BOOK 6 — 139

Watch Your Mouth — 142
Just Things — 149
The Act of Love — 151

BOOK 7	**157**
Love	158
Fresh Start	170
God's Love in Everything from The Beginning	171
BOOK 8	**179**
The Most Insane of People Can Be Used to Help Us All Get to That Better Place	183
Time and Chaos	185
Why all the F**king Pain?	189
Getting Little, Getting Low	194
It's That Simple. It's The Same Thing. We Make it More Difficult	197
Open Up	200
Seven Gifts of the Spririt	202
Surrender	206
Gifts of Love	209
Good Suffering	210
Let Go. Let God.	213
Circumstances	215
God's Waiting for Us	222
More Control	227
God Doesn't Gamble	228
A Miracle	231
Miracles Through Man	232
Man's Law vs. God's Law	238
Childlike	250
More Kid Stuff	253
How Childish. Exactly.	256

Change, Change, Change.	259
What's Up?	262
So If Nothing Changes, Nothing Changes	264
Grace. Check This Out	268
Faith. Check This Out	268
One Nation Under God	270
BOOK A-Z	273
Final Thoughts	304
Conclusions	309
Epilogue	311
Acknowledgements	312

This book is dedicated to Dena, my mother, who loved me unconditionally. She always told me to "Look up, not down." She was the most wonderful, patient and saintly person I've ever known and I miss her every day. As she looks upon me from Heaven, I want her to know that I understand and "get" what she was telling me and will try my very best each and every day to make her proud.

This book is also dedicated to Judy, my girlfriend and the love of my life. We met over twenty years ago at a small dance studio. Her wisdom and patience has inspired me and I want her to know I will try my very best each and every day to be the man she can count on.

This book is also dedicated to anyone who has allowed their issues and demons to prevent them from hearing God's message and receiving His love. It is never too late to heal, and it is never too late to do the right thing.

Prologue

I go to bed in a man-made prison and bondage, tired, empty.

My strength poured out in, oh so many years of tears shed for so much. Some sorrows, but mainly for frustrations, confusions, inability and pain…so much pain, resentment and anger.

So tired, I lie and rest, fake true sleep in the darkness. A darkness that is welcomed over reality in a place where flies won't land. This dark, empty, lonely cell of lies and life.

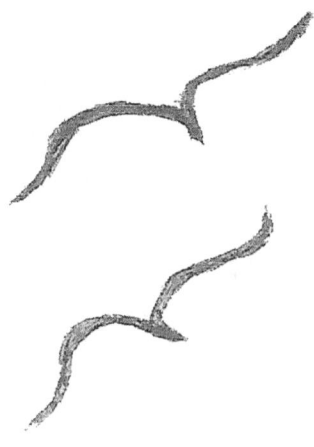

Book 1

God's Way

Beat the Beast by God's thinking and wisdom—not ours!

I say don't get into it with the dude and don't even bother arguing with him either; he's been at this a very, very long time.

Jesus lets us know that Satan only comes for one reason demonstrated in three ways. This is what Jesus says in John 10:10, "Satan comes to KILL, to STEAL and to DESTROY." You might as well be ready and trust me the devil is good at this. These three things have been his specialty since God put him out of the big house. "How you have fallen from Heaven" (Isaiah 14:12). If you're not extremely careful, if you misjudge him or ease up a little, or don't take him seriously he can destroy you!

God says, "Be wise as serpents and as harmless as doves" (Matthew 10:16).

The beast who easily has preyed on our innocent ignorance. I say innocent because how do you defend what you are too young to understand? Innocence because the beast can only devour when we rely on our own understandings and strengths, and self-centeredness is inescapable in our infant years because it is how we survive and live. However, the beast has little abilities where there is only one. It is when there is more involved, two, three, many, that the beast makes its moves, finagling, conniving, lying, and manipulating its way into our ultimate destruction if it can. As the numbers grow, its influence on man seems more appealing to man and it casts more and more evil. Throughout the many years of my discoveries I have learned many things about the beast or shark. I see the things in people that the beast loves to rely on to meet its needs. Things like strong bodies, loud voices, and quick thinkers. Now I know some of this is beyond my natural understanding of how some of this spiritual stuff works, but I know and guarantee you, I will believe and trust in what God has given me to use and understand.

My Peaceful Work

One thing I learned is that Satan has and will use all faces. One of his best tricks, outside of my own weaknesses, was to come at me in the form of another Christian. Yes, another Christian. So be cool and listen here. The devil will use whatever he can. Religion, circumstances, job, relationships, women, men, money, economy, family, friends. You may not even know who's doing it. So, now listen to what I have to say. If you don't take heed and fight with the thinking and knowledge of God, Satan will succeed in taking away everything good in your life.

Now take a deep breath and start to find the comfort in knowing God has promised me and promised you all this. If you will continue to pursue and get to know God and God's love you will experience positive spiritual growth and you will change for the better. Guaranteed! If you pursue this growing in love, get to know Jesus better, and God better, allowing them to love you as you pursue loving them back, I know for sure you will be well on your way to fulfilling your divine calls as it unfolds!

To those people who are prideful, arrogant types, self-centered types and those virtuous types possessing selfishness and greed, I've found myself many, many times in the beast's clutches due to my bad choices and actions. I could go on and on but I want to get to the solution and not dwell so much on the problem. I believe we all know about the problem so I'll elaborate a little further, then move on. By striking or influencing the right person, the right mind, the beast could end us all, just like that. It all starts with a thought – more on this later. But the more I thought about it, I asked myself why? Why? How stupid would that be? Does the beast not realize that the end of mankind is also his <u>final</u> destruction – his destruction?

Now dawn comes. Light shines in a place with no light switch, no windows, and yet I see having been truly emptied. You see you have to be emptied one way or the other to be refilled or replenished with something better. I hope so for the beast and I have fought so hard even he must rest. Now I may lay aside my little weapons, grabbing hold of the true source of my powers and strengths and finally give thought and expression as to what I'm supposed to do. My peaceful work.

I Choose Love

PRETTY POISON

You're like a diamond sparkling in the sand

And your beauty can catch the eye of any man.

Yet you're so cold and so appealing,

You took away my soul, my feeling.

Your passions imprisoned me,

And made me blind to your reality.

I should have seen the demon in your eyes

Behind all the pretty smiles and all the f*cking lies.

Author: Frank

With a New Day

WITH A NEW DAY I AM GIVEN A NEW TRY

I've always been rushing and running,

Running, running – from it all – then stumbling in a fog.

Then off a cliff, back up, off yet another - still falling - falling.

Back up – falling again, so very close to the ending, the bottom.

So now be aware, he who pushes me further, "Beware!"

For now it's time for me (and all of those who choose to read this) to FIGHT BACK.

You lose beast!

Author: Frank

I was going to start this book talking about myself, my life experiences, many of which were not so pleasant, but for some reason I just couldn't get started. Then it became clear as I have been in situations where, let's just say I was able to do a lot of reading. Much more than I ever wanted to. Yet, in doing so I have been truly blessed with the opportunities to learn from the smartest people in the world. I've read many self-help books, spiritual books, books about psychology. The list is endless. These authors and scholars are much smarter than me and I'll try my best to acknowledge them throughout this book and within my attempts to put into words all I have learned from them. You see, I look at it this way. Life should be like a relay race. You don't start over from the beginning, you go on from where they pass you the baton. The same is true for people. We learn from adults, our parents, teachers, clergy, and others and we should pass on our experiences, hopes, strengths and knowledge. Yet today it seems to be falling on deaf ears. Kids today are getting worse. They are not listening. They are not hearing or just not getting any true positive guidance. I have put some of my experiences in this book in order to grow and gain some very important truths. This, however, may not happen with some kids today. Some, if not many, will die in the streets not knowing the truth. It is my hope that even if it's just one kid who reads this and gets it, well then I was right to share it and pass it on. That one kid will make it all worth it. My hope is that if you read this book you will come to understand the basic key formulas to life and the answer to the question – "What is the meaning of life?"

What's the Meaning of Life?

My name is Frank and I'm a recovering person. I'm not going to get into all the details of my life and this is not going to be a rags-to-riches type of book, at least not in the financial sense of that phrase. This book will just simply change your life for the better. Guaranteed. No question about it. I will, however, disclose some personal information about myself. Simply put, I've been around—business owner, entertainer, dancer, choreographer, party animal, drug addict, thief. From the penthouse to the jailhouse, from sailing coast to coast to outrunning cops in a yacht. Seen it all. Been there. Done that. I'm not going to elaborate so we can get to the solutions. The problems are many and obvious to us. Isn't that why you picked up this book? The formula to life and the meaning of life? I want to ask one favor to all who read this and that is if you get something out of this book as I'm sure you will, please pass this book on or recommend it to two other people, and let's see if together we can make a little difference in this crowded, confused, and turbulent world we live in.

THE STARFISH STORY

One day a man was walking along the beach when he noticed a boy picking something up and gently throwing it into the ocean.

Approaching the boy, he asked, "What are you doing?"

The youth replied, "Throwing the starfish back into the ocean. The surf is up and the tide is going out. If I don't throw them back, they'll die."

"Son." the man said, "Don't you realize there are miles of beach and hundreds of starfish? You can't make a difference!"

After listening politely, the boy bent down, picked up another starfish and threw it back into the surf.

Then smiling at the man he said, "I made a difference for that one."

Author: Loren Eiseley

As long as we are breathing, after we learn let's pass our new baton off to others. Be careful and hurry because crime, drugs, gangs, violence, evil and corruption is getting worse, right?

Before we move on, I would like you to pay close attention to the common denominator. All the words that follow come together and work together for one purpose. One true purpose only.

To get us jump started here, let's start with what drives us most.

Resentments

Resentments are Number One.

Most of us, at one time or another, have been hurt badly and for some reason we don't seem to get over it, right? Or is it that we really don't want to get over it? You are probably thinking, why would I not want to get over someone or something that has hurt me badly?

My father left us when I was seven years old. I've witnessed and experienced some pretty awful things prior to and through this all. And let's just say I held onto this resentment (anger) for a very long time. As a matter of fact, I fed it and nourished it so I could continue to use it as an excuse to do what I really wanted to do anyway. I used my resentment as an excuse to do drugs and f**k off because that's really what I wanted to do in the first place. Hell, it was easier than dealing with all the pain, right? Wrong! Not in the long run! Some people deal with anger and resentment by stifling their true feelings and holding them inside. Some blow up on others using violence. Neither work. They are unhealthy and solve nothing. Instead it creates consequences for others who may not even know about your issues or resentments, or the reasons behind them.

Bottom line? Resentment hurts you more than the person who hurt you. Those who hurt you can only keep hurting you if you allow it and hold onto the pain.

Fear Driven

Many of our fears come from drama or a bad experience. One of my fears is the fear of abandonment. Of course this stems from my childhood issues. Regardless of the cause of our fear, if we continue to be afraid to take chances because we dread getting hurt again, we are going to "miss the boat" in life. We are not going to fully live our lives. We play it safe. I ran from most of my relationships in life because of this resentment and fear of abandonment. Using drugs also is a form of running. Generally it's running from emotional pain. The point I'm trying to make is that it is foolish to continue to worry and fret over the resentments in our lives. We need to move toward a well-formed love, and against anger and resentment. A well-formed love banishes fear. Fear of life or death is a life not yet understanding or formed by God in love.

FOOTPRINTS

One night I had a dream. I dreamed I was walking along the beach with the Lord. Across the sky flashed scenes from my life. For each scene I noticed two sets of footprints in the sand; one belonging to me and the other to the Lord.

When the last scene of my life flashed before me, I looked back at the footprints in the sand. I noticed that many times along the path of my life there was only one set of footprints.

I also noticed that it happened at the very lowest and saddest times in my life.

This really bothered me and I questioned the Lord about it.

"Lord, I noticed that at times my footprints seemed to go all over the place, back and forth, left and right, up and down – everywhere and sometimes all at once."

I was all over the place (running/seeking trying to learn and find life's answers).

So again I asked about the one set of prints and the Lord told me that's when he carried me.

I asked about when the footprints were all over the place and He said "my child, that's when we danced."

Author: A variation of the original poem by Mary Stevenson

Money (Greed)

For many of us our desire to acquire becomes everything in life. We put it ahead of all that we love or what we should be loving, and this then makes us want more and more. And then we believe or start to believe we can only be happy with more and more. But this is not true. Materialistic things are only very temporary, brief forms of happiness at best. You will not become more important. You will not become happier. People will not love you more. They may, however, love the materialistic things you can give for the moment. Real security comes from that which cannot be taken from you.

Approval (trying to fit in)

Unrealistic expectations of self, peer pressure, always worried what others think, trying to please everyone. How's this list so far? When I was lost in greed with things/toys, I tried to fill it with drugs and sex. When I was young, we moved around so much I went to nine different schools and I tried to fit in any way I could. I was the class clown. I was the guy who would always take a dare. I had no long term friends or buddies because I was always moving. Relationships? Forget it. I didn't trust that. Truly open up to anything or anybody? Forget it. Not me. It hurts too much if you do. I now can see patterns and all the life choices I've made up to this point had to do with those feelings of resentment.

In order to live the lifestyle I wanted, which was not dealing with anything real, it was easier just to party. The restaurant business and the nightclubs I ran or worked at, the entertainment business, dancing, choreography, all of it was a party lifestyle. All phony. One big party that eventually would and could not last. All to fill the void of one simple thing. Love. There's that word again. I remember sitting on the apartment steps or the porch every night as a child waiting for my dad to come home but he never did. I remember feelings of being different from other people and their families. Who will go to parent/teacher conferences at school? Who will teach me how to play sports, defend myself in a fight, or tell me about girls? How do I learn to be a man? Well, I learned in all the wrong places, trust me. I learned in the pool halls, in the streets, in the party atmosphere, jail, and other places.

Whatever the source of your resentment, the results are the same when handled inappropriately. Whatever the source of your pain, be it bad relationships, wasted abilities, stress, changes, unfulfilled dreams, pointlessness, pettiness, resentment, anger, fear, money problems, greed, pride, lust, in order to overcome, there must be forgiveness and love.

NO FEAR

I love you more than life itself, but I'm afraid to love

My heart is like the fragile wings of a tiny dove.

I'm scared to get too close, I feel that I can't win

You'll love me for a while, then you'll set me free again.

I've lived so long on hopes and dreams; I don't know what to do.

I don't think I can trust my heart for it belongs to you.

I know you'll only hurt me yet I still keep running back

Between the paths of our hearts there's a worn and beaten track.

You got my heart held on a string; it's breaking right in two.

Enough belongs to me to hurt, the rest belongs to you.

Know that somewhere in your heart there is a place for me.

I just don't know how to find it and there's no way to make you see.

I can only hope that one day we wake up and find

That while my heart belongs to yours, yours too belongs to mine.

Author: Unknown

Let's talk a little more about fear because I know from experience that this isn't going to go away easily and the devil will get all over it if you let him.

"There is no fear in love, but perfect love casteth out fear; because fear hath torment. He that feareth is not made perfect in love" (1 John 4:18).

We may be cruising along life's road just fine and dandy. Okay in our faith, trusting God and confident that God loves us. Then all of a sudden here comes the devil. Some of the things I've mentioned in these first pages pop up or bad things start to happen that tests our faith. Sometimes (initially) it may even seem hopeless or unbelievable, right? You see most of us don't have trouble believing there is a God who loves us especially when things are going okay, but how about when things don't look so good? Here comes the devil (The Beast) with fear, old memories and resentments. Trying anything to throw us off. Trying to take us away from the only thing, (I said the only thing) the very thing that will help you and that is God's "love."

Pay attention. The devil will come at you with self-talk using fear, doubts and other things. It's not fair, is it? How often have you said, "If God loves us, then how is this crap happening to me, especially now after all the good I've done?" How often have you thought to yourself that you're just dumb, useless and awful? "God doesn't love me, He's mad at me." When life seems unfair it is easy to lose some, if not all of your confidence. Don't lose your confidence. You see God does not think like we do and that's a good thing. If God thought like us it really would be a screwed up world. He always, always has a plan that's far better than ours could ever be. I believe that God is usually working on us as people more than any and all circumstances surrounding us. He's working on fixing us and changing us for the better. I believe He has used most of the pain in my life to drive me to becoming more dependent on Him alone. I'm sure He's doing the same with you.

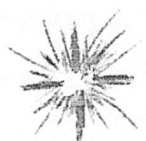

Book 2

Worry

When we overcome our fear with faith, that's how God makes our worries into worship.

So let go and let God. During these trying times when we don't understand what is happening we can easily slip into the devil's trap that starts with our thinking that God does not love us. But know that the Bible says in Romans 8:35, "We should never allow anything to separate us from the love of God that is found in Jesus Christ." God is never too late!

There is a story in the Bible about Jesus helping a family—a man named Lazarus and Martha, his sister. Lazarus was dying. Jesus went to their house and Martha told Him, "You are too late. My brother is dead." Jesus then raised Lazarus from the dead right then and there. God is never too late! When you're dazed, confused and having difficulties in your life, keep your faith. Don't fear. Don't doubt. Don't let anything steal the love of God from you.

The Bible says in John 4:18, "Perfect love casts out fear." Know this that God's love is that love. God's love for you is perfect and when we finally get this, understand this—just how great, how perfect God's love is toward us, then nothing, and I mean nothing, can control you or me. You will not let fear, anger or resentment control you. Although you may feel things like fear you will keep stepping towards God.

Turn the other cheek. Walk away. Take a time-out. Surrender. Give up everything to start fresh. Let go and let God. No fear. No doubt.

Know also that when you do let go, it will be impossible to fear anything for long if you know that God loves you! He loves you and He loved you first and foremost. He loved you first. You're now free to grow in all areas of life. Try things with the comfort in knowing that God's love, His appreciation and His acceptance is not based on what you do or how good you are at it. You can't, I repeat, you can't fail if you depend on God. The only way we will fail (you and I) is if we rely or depend on ourselves or others. Like man or dope, or anything for that matter, if you put your expectations on others or anything but God you will eventually be let down (we're all only human). If you know God's love and accept that He loves you, you cannot lack for anything. The past can't hurt. The future will not be feared. There is no rejection or failure. God's love is so great it covers everything. Why? Because He created everything. Simple, right?

Keep It Simple Stupid

First I must say to myself, Frank, keep it simple stupid. I have participated in and run numerous AODA programs. I even developed some modules for a program or two. I've also read like a vacuum almost everything written on the subject of psychology 101-104. I'm Ok, You're Ok by Dr. Thomas A. Harris, books by Dr. Sigmund Freud, Inside the Criminal Mind by Dr. Stanley Sameno and participated in groups, AA, NA, CA, Transactional analysis, and all kinds of therapies. Group, shock, confrontational, and others. I have also participated in all types of programs. Smart Recovery, Cognitive Thinking, Power of Positive Thinking, all of it faith-based, as well as meditation and yoga. The list is endless.

I'm telling you all this for a reason. All these books and therapies were helpful. All were wonderful. All had a purpose and I truly was looking for something else in life so that's why I took part in these therapeutic groups and programs, to figure it all out. What makes me tick? What's the answer to the big question? What's life all about? So when I use the popular AA term "keep it simple stupid" it is because my intellect kept me sick a long time. I allowed this. Example: the very first words of AA (Alcoholics Anonymous) is we admitted we were alcoholics. I would then take the simple word "admitted" and dissect it into a million particles just to prove it did not apply to me. I did this with everything.

So just keep that in mind. Now here's my simple question for you.

Do you think that the same God who saved you and set you free is now going to make you feel like a failure? Will He leave you helpless? Is that what you think? Well, of course not.

Satan is the enemy of our souls. Satan is a thief and a liar, but Jesus wants us to have and enjoy life. The Bible says in 1 John 4:18, "There is no fear in love. But full-grown love turns fear out of doors and expels every trace of terror!" No doubt. No fear. Let go. Let God. Keep it simple stupid.

No guilt, shame, hurt, resentments or running as we begin growing into God's love for us.

We need to keep growing into God's love of complete perfection.

We have to let God love us and then love Him back. How do we do this? One thing I learned in my life's research has to do with habit. What is a habit? Webster's Dictionary says "an often involuntary pattern of behavior acquired by frequent repetition."

After I quit smoking I realized this. The way I acquired the habit of smoking was by doing it all the time until it became a habit. So to stop, to try something new or different, I had to practice something new to change it. So I made myself say no. Do you smoke? No. Would you like a cigarette? No. Care for a cigarette? No. No. No. I did this long enough and it became a habit to just say no to cigarettes once and for all. An interesting thing then happened. After saying no enough the people who were asking moved on as well.

Practice something long enough until it becomes a habit. Like saying no.

Now that we have this new knowledge about God's love for us (He loved us first) and that we need to love Him back, let's put this knowledge into practice. Do it often enough that it becomes a habit. We have to let God love us, we have to let God love us. Repeat after me. We have to let God love us.

You Had it all Along

KEY TO MY HEART

I had closed the door upon my heart and wouldn't let anyone in,
I had trusted and loved only to be hurt, but that would never happen again,
I had locked the door and tossed the keys as hard and as far as I could
Love would never enter there again, my heart was closed for good.
Then You came into my life and made me change my mind
Just when I thought that tiny key was impossible to find
That's when You held out Your hand and proved to me I was wrong
Inside Your palm (with the hole) was the key to my heart.
You had it all along.

Author: Amanda Marie

"And if I go and prepare a place for you, I will come again, and receive you unto myself; that where I am, there ye may be also" (John 14:3).

Cause and Effect

He is coming, oh the rapture
To behold the lovely fall
And to tell Him how I love Him
Who has saved me by His grace.

Author: Dimmock

Did you know the love of God controlled Jesus?

"As the Father has loved Me, so have I loved you. Now remain in My love" (John 15:9).

Remember the effect of something, anything, is never greater than its cause. Life and nature live by this law.

Examples:
- ✓ The brilliance of the sun is not greater than the sun.
- ✓ My salvation is not greater than the Creator.
- ✓ The creation is not greater than the Creator.
- ✓ A house is not greater than the builder.

Get it? I knew you would.

Head Trip

You've got to let God. I mean you've got to let it all go. Total surrender. Let it go. Move around!

I had to learn all this some very hard ways. I'm still learning. I won't get into all the details, so just trust me on this. I had to literally beat myself into surrender. And even today I let stuff go, give it to God and then grab it right back. I analyzed it over and over, then I worry about it over and over. I have to keep practicing daily so you may have a little trouble with some of this as well, but if we remember to keep practicing it until it becomes a habit, we'll be okay. We all must stop trying to outthink Him! Don't forget one of my biggest obstacles and I believe the number one obstacle we all face is ourselves. Remember I told you how I allowed my intellect to keep me sick for a long time? I always out-thought and dissected every issue to come up with what I thought were the right solutions, or to prove that something did not apply to me. Rather than keep it simple and trust the Spirit, I ended up with quick fixes or partial solutions. It is kind of like taking a hit of dope. The Spirit would try to give me a couple of free passes or give me a sign but I kept analyzing what was true or feasible and thus, could not make any progress. I believe there are two different frequencies, so to speak. The Spirit knows things that your head does not know. 1 Corinthians 2:14 says, "But the natural man receiveth not the things of the Spirit of God; for they are foolishness unto him; neither can he know them, because they are spiritually discerned."

Deception

If you don't want to be deceived then I found there is only one way to even come close to preventing it and that is not to be led by anything in the flesh. Those of us who are led by their own thinking, our "head trips" and our emotions, or our own will rather than by God's word or will, can and will, yes I said will, be deceived! I like no unanswered questions. I like to put every detail in its proper place. I always try to figure every angle and every current and potential future problem, but because of this additional form of thinking – you guessed it, it took me even longer to get to where I'm even at now. So the smarter I was really only made me dumber, why? Because God used this to get me to finally see the truth and in doing so through all my unanswered questions. You see if I couldn't get it on my own, or from anyone else, I then finally had to trust God, or keep struggling and worrying and try to figure it out on my own. Trust me. Enough pain and you will surrender. Now God has your attention!

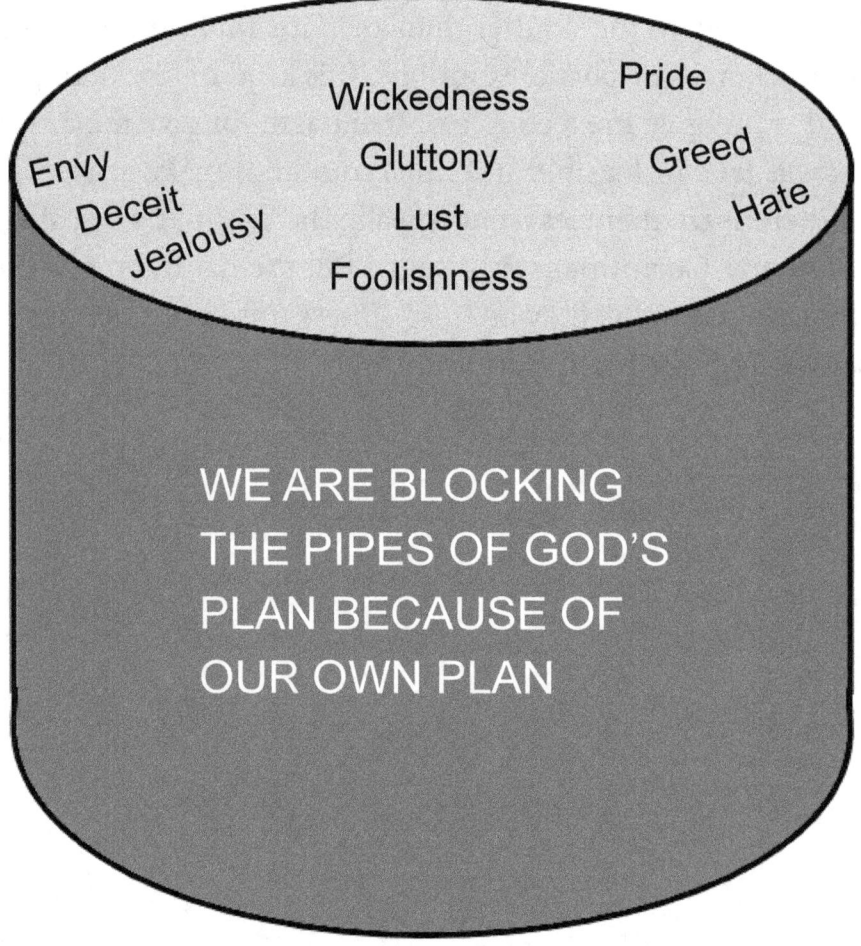

And more importantly we have all this time to make a good choice before it becomes a function.

Lean on, trust in, and be confident in the Lord with all your heart and mind and do not rely on your own insight or understanding. In all your ways know, recognize and acknowledge Him, and He will direct and make straight and plain your paths.

One other thing that I learned is if it is "of God" or "God's plan" you will experience no confusion or doubt.

Watch What You Ask For, You Just Might Get It

Know this about God. God is a patient God. Time means nothing to Him and He will repeat the lessons over and over and over until we get it.

Child of a deathless morn

You were not ever born

You will not ever die

For time is mind's ancient lie

Its fleeting fancy's pass

Across minds looking glass

Forever old and new

No child of time are you

But through eternity

You are and will be

And have the meaning whole

Already in your soul.

Author: Frank

I say watch what you ask for because, for example, if you pray for more patience where better to learn how to be patient than perhaps a prison cell for maybe 10-15 years or more? That is one place to learn all about patience, right? Or, if you pray for love; how can we understand love if we don't fully understand hate? So to learn love God may choose to put you around a whole lot of hate first so you finally learn to fully appreciate love.

Realize that our own insights mean very little at times. The best example is this: I remember two stories, one of which was in the Bible. Those two stories were very similar, but had the opposite results by God. Polycarp (69-155 AD) was a bishop. Roman authorities asked him to curse Christ if he wanted to be released. He had served Christ 86 years and said, "How can I blaspheme my King that saved me?" The Romans threatened to have him consumed with fire if he did not change his mind. Polycarp remained firm and did not curse Christ. He was burned at the stake.

Around 600 BC, three men, Shadrach, Meshach and Abednego, were brought before King Nebuchadnezzar. They were threatened with a fiery death unless they cursed Christ. Prior to entering the furnace, the three men told the Romans the same thing. "Let it be known to you O King we do not serve your Gods." These three men left the burning furnace unsinged. Not a mark on them.

Same faith. Two very different results by God. What's my point? God is God. Faith in God is not just faith in what He can do. He has the first say and the final say. We need to stop trying to figure it all out with our simple human understandings because that keeps us from joy, peace and God's love. Rest your assurances on God's love in your heart and not on the fears in your mind.

Understand this. I'm still weak at times. I know I am getting much better acquainted with God's love and my understanding of it but I still worry at times, and I still fear at times. So it's clear I too have to continue to grow in my understanding of God's love. I'm sure when I know, when we know how much God loves us the fear, worries and concerns will all disappear. It has to! God wants to bless us so much we can't even comprehend it. He wants us to be victorious over all areas of our lives and He wants to give us all joy and get and give His love over and over, continuously every second by second in every situation.

"Perfect love casts out fear" (John 4:48). And God is that perfect love.

God really does know what He is doing, ok? He really is in control. That much is now clearly obvious to me. How about you? So we can start to chill out a little. I may not know at times who I truly am or where I'm truly going all the time, but I do know the One who does. I don't know about you, but I've wasted far too much time trying to hold on to all the wrong s*it, and trying to figure it out – all the wasted time in confusion and fear and worry. Hey, why don't you and I try this? What if we just chill out here? Be cool and let God be God. Let go, let God.

From the Beginning

It's never been about man vs. man or about man vs. self. It's always been about "God and Man."

Hang in there. God's love for us will work it out, in and through us, for sure. Many people believe they are not good enough or worthy. All of us may not seem to fit in, but God loves us and will love us to the highest level if we love Him back, accept the love He has for us and stop making excuses.

Some of the most mentioned people in the Bible had excuses and issues. Saul was a religious terrorist who persecuted and conspired to kill Christians. After his conversion, he became known as Paul and was a powerful figure who shared the Gospel of Jesus. He was imprisoned and suffered from poor health.

Abraham lied about his relationship with his wife. Jacob was a deceiver who had low self-esteem. Joseph was a victim of abuse. Moses was a murderer and had a hot temper. Gideon was a victim of poverty. David committed adultery with Bathsheba. Rahab was a prostitute. Samson was vengeful, a womanizer and a murderer. John the Baptist was bold and fearless, almost to the point of arrogance. Peter was rash and restless and imprisoned. Martha suffered from anxiety and worry. Elijah suffered from bouts of depression. Jonah was a stubborn, disobedient and grumbling old man. Timothy was shy and faithful, but also scared. Thomas struggled with doubt. The Samaritan woman at the well was immoral and ostracized by her people for openly living with a series of men though unmarried. Leah was homely and jealous of her sister's beauty.

Adding myself and all of you makes this quite a list. God shows us through these examples that He loves us through our weaknesses and imperfections.

Whatever your demons, pain or sorrows, hang in there. Keep stepping toward God and He will work it out in time. The right time. Guaranteed!

Weakness

If God only had righteous people to choose from He would have no one to choose or pick! When I was a kid, I used to run up the down escalators at the shopping malls. Maybe you have done this as well. Do you remember? As the escalator is going down, you have to keep pushing yourself and pushing yourself to go up, and if you stop or even rest for a split second, you end up going back down backwards. Recovery, growth, positive change, letting God love you and loving God back are all just like this. We have to keep pressing forward no matter what, okay? Bottom line, we're born in sin. We're all just plain sinners and there's nothing we can do about it by ourselves. It is only through God's love for us and the sacrifice of His son Jesus that we have His love. It is not because of anything we did or could do. What an awesome example of His love for us.

God also uses what the world considers to be weak people. Your own weaknesses are not an accident either. The Bible is full of examples of how God loves to use imperfect people, the ordinary people to do the extraordinary things in spite of the weaknesses. If God only used perfect people nothing would get done because none of us are flawless. You need to understand this. God uses our weaknesses so he can demonstrate His Love and power through those weaknesses in us. And please dig this as well. You are who and what you are for a reason and part of an intricate plan. God's plan. Dig this as we are all fixable because we're products of a superior mastermind. God loves you unconditionally.

Agape Love

"Who shall separate us from the love of Christ? Shall tribulations, distress or persecution, or famine or nakedness or peril or sword? As it is written for thy sake, we are killed all the day long; we are accounted as sheep for the slaughter" (Psalm 44:22).

"Nay in all these things we are more than conquerors through Him that loved us. For I am persuaded that neither death nor life, nor angels, nor principalities, nor powers, nor things present, nor things to come, nor height or depth nor any other creature, shall be able to separate us from the Love of God which is in Christ Jesus our Lord" (Romans 8:35-39).

So please get this now. It is only as we are filled to the measures with the fullness of God's love for us that we will "bear" true fruit of love for others.

Note we cannot love properly or completely or fully in our own strength.

Always remember God is the initiator. We can love because He first loved us.

We are the responders. "This is love: not that we loved God but that He loved us and sent his Son as an atoning sacrifice for our sins" (1 John 4:10).

RAINDROPS

Raindrop after raindrop and day after day
The sky sheds the tears that I thought were hid away
Occasional thunder rumbles through the night
Venting the rage that I hide in morning's light
Brilliant bolts of lightning flash in my head
Visions of you holding me as we tremble in my bed.
Raindrop after raindrop and day after day
The sky sheds the tears for a love so close
Yet so far away.

Author: Frank

John said, "God is Love" (John 4:16).

If what I now know is the beginning of the answer to what life is all about then what could be more important right now than to learn more about it, or aim to learn how to live in this God-kind of love. I want to know each and everything I can about it. Oh yes, I am familiar with the other kinds of love and "supposed" love out there. Webster's Dictionary defines a few: "Love: intense affection (a) feeling of attraction resulting from sexual desire, (b) enthusiasm or fondness. Love of music/a beloved person. To enjoy enthusiastically."

We all kind of get this sort of love you know. It can be strong like some of our youthful crushes, or even the feeling like when a girl first touched my private part. Hell I thought that was all love was about, but you see, the love we get has mostly its own interests at stake. It's like this—I'll love you as long as somehow love can, or you can keep giving me what I want or brings me some kind of pleasure. Most of us know how to love this way or conditionally, but we do not or aren't very good at walking in this kind of Agape love.

"Agape love" – let's check Webster's Dictionary again. <u>"Christian love—love that is spiritual not sexual. With wonder and amazement—wide open."</u> Anyway, I believe this Agape love is a type of self-denying love. Its total focus is always in the interest of the other party or of the person you are loving.

Regular love: I might go to war (enlist) because of pride in the USA.

Agape love: Will go with a different motivation, like to instill peace for all.

Said another way, most relationships that end up in a marriage are based on regular love. The people love each other based on what they get out of it or what they receive from each other. If all marriages were based on the kind of love I'm trying to explain, God's selfless kind of love, divorce would not exist. Get it. God is Love. God not only loves us, but God is Love. Period. It would be impossible for God not to love us. Now get this as well. This is why we haven't even come close to understanding Him the way we should. "Be thou merciful even as your Father also is merciful" (John 6:36). How merciful? Well try this on. You and I were completely lost going straight to Hell. You know we were completely bankrupt, tapped out, nothing to begin to even bargain with. Not only could we not come to God, step toward Him, beg or reach out to Him, we had no chips. We were not and still are not capable of closing the gap on our own. But God had the love for all of us and the mercy we didn't have coming, didn't deserve and could not begin to even earn. God chose to come to us once again in His mercy and love for us. He crossed and closed the hole, the void with Jesus' blood.

Remember I said earlier that when we learn to practice something new long enough that it becomes a habit? Well, Jesus gave us some guidelines on how to start to do this in Luke 6:27-38 which says, "But I tell you who hear me: Love your enemies, do good to those who hate you, bless those who curse you. If someone strikes you on one cheek, turn to him the other also. If someone takes your cloak, do not stop him from taking your tunic. Give to everyone who asks you, and if anyone takes what belongs to you, do not demand it back. Do to others as you would have them do to you. If you love those who love you, what credit is that to you? Even 'sinners' love those who love them. And if you do good to those who are good to you, what credit is that to you? Even 'sinners' do that. And if you lend to those from whom you expect repayment, what credit is that to you? Even 'sinners' lend to 'sinners', expecting to be repaid in full. But love your enemies, do good to them and lend to them without expecting to get anything back. Then your reward will be great, and you will be sons of the Most High, because He is kind to the ungrateful and wicked. Be merciful just as your Father is merciful. Do not judge, and you will not be judged. Do not condemn, and you will not be condemned. Forgive, and you will be forgiven."

In this way, we are now practicing the mercy God gives us all the time, every single day. What is the result of this kind of love? Luke goes on to say in 6:38, "Give, and it will be given to you. A good measure, pressed down shaken together and running over, will be poured into your lap. For with the measure you use, it will be measured to you."

I believe what Jesus was saying here is this. If you will be children of God and give Agape love to others then God will restore any and all you may lose plus. If you get ripped off because of trying or giving mercy, then God will give back overflowing all you lost. Now concentrate and understand this. This is why God's love cannot and will not fail!

Because of the way we are this will not always be an easy thing to do, especially in this world today. And it's not getting better or easier to show this special love when sin and hate are everywhere.

The line in the following diagram is God's plan for us from (a) to (b). A straight perfect line. Our defects is the other line through this life.

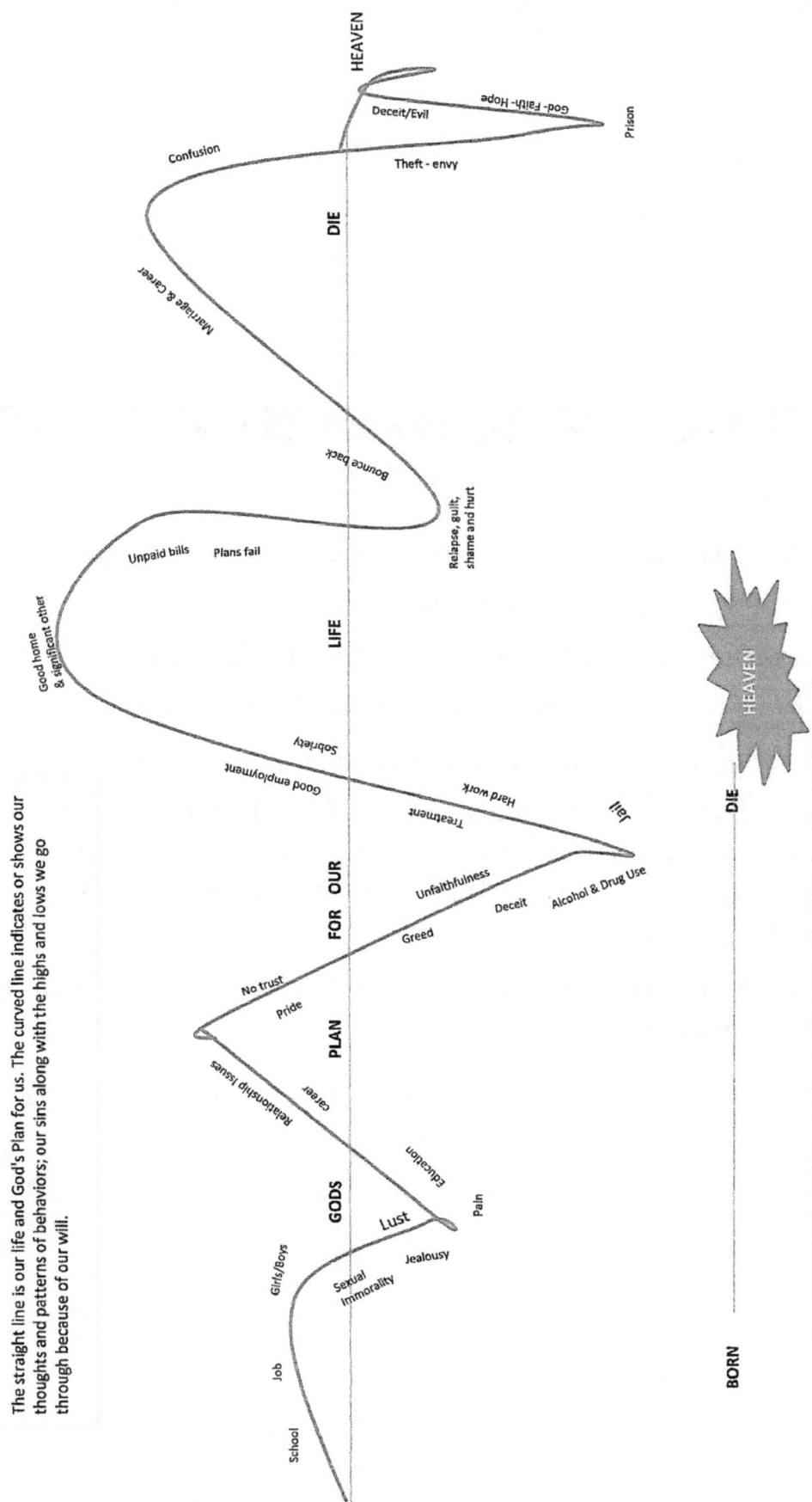

FOOTPRINTS

One night I dreamed I was walking along the beach with the Lord.

Many scenes from my life flashed across the sky.

In each sometimes there were two sets of footprints, other times there was only one.

This bothered me because I noticed that during the low periods of my life, when

I was suffering from anguish, sorrow or doubt, I could only see one set of footprints.

So I said to the Lord "you promised me Lord that if I followed you, you would walk with me always. But I have noticed that during the most trying periods of my life there has only been one set of footsteps in the sand. Why, when I needed you most, have you not been there for me?"

The Lord replied, "The years where you have only seen one set of footprints, my child, is when I carried you."

Author: Mary Stevenson

The Force of Love

God did not create the bullsh*t in our lives. We did. Understand, that as we start to practice this new kind of love together this other crap will fall away. A little at a time perhaps, but it will fall away and as we get better and better at it, it will get closer and closer to God's plan as shown on the diagram.

Stick to God's plan and instructions and keep our bullsh*t out of it and we get farther faster, and much smoother.

Even though God has planted the nature and force of agape love in all our spirits it may be almost non-existent because of our emotions and fears. But when you pray and keep walking up the down escalator toward God, and as we stay closer to His line, His plan for us, we bypass a lot of the bullsh*t and the edification process starts to grow the seeds of God's love, Agape love in our hearts. Therefore, it must continue to grow. It must.

This force of love in you, in us all, will grow more and more and get bigger and bigger until one day it takes over all our past negative emotions and we then become new. We become new!

"That ye put off concerning the former conversation (the old man), which is corrupt according to deceitful lusts, and be renewed in the spirit of your mind and that ye put on the new man, which after God is created in righteousness and true holiness" Ephesians (4:22-24).

Now we're getting somewhere here, aren't we? We can do this and I think we're finding the meaning of life here!

Remember what was said about fear in previous pages. Here's how we know we're growing and getting closer, and how we know this love is being perfected in us. "Perfect love cast out fear, for fear has torment" (1 John 4:18). So when we see the crap fall away from us and let go of all the worries, fear, torment and confusion, we'll be more at peace. Trust me, you'll see, feel and know the difference. The same sh*t won't bother you like it used to. Then you'll know that love is being perfected in you!

Here is a quick example just to drive this home a little further.

If you decide to rob me, how could I extend mercy if I had fear, torment or resentments about it? But when and as this love is being perfected in me, I know it's going to be ok because you can take all I have at the time, but Luke 6:38 says, "That my Father is going to restore it all back to me" and give me more to boot! Don't forget we know this because as we will shed fear and torments, peace will take over. The peace will dominate more and more as we practice. Paul says in Corinthians 12:31, "And now I will show you the most excellent way." If you want to save yourself a lot of trouble then you need to covet this kind of agape love with everything in you the same way you covet the best gifts. Just how important is pursuing agape love? Paul makes this additional statement in 1 Corinthians 13:13, "and now abideth faith, hope and love, these three, but the greatest of these is love!"

I believe most of the best scholars would say that faith would be the most important or the greatest thing here and then maybe hope. Hope is the time alone you spend reading or studying God's Word. Your doing this is hope. That you get it, which causes your faith to grow and manifest. But Paul says and I believe this to be the answer we're looking for is that greater than faith and greater than hope is self-denying Agape love. That means there is nothing more important in your life to covet and earnestly desire than agape love.

The Goal is Agape Love

Are you ready for even a little more proof that this love thing we're talking about is truly the greatest truth to the meaning of life, our life?

Paul, a pretty sharp dude, right—biggest contributor of the Bible by the way—says in 1 Corinthians 13:8, "Love never faileth: but whether there be prophecies they shall fail; whether there be tongues, they shall cease; whether there be knowledge, it shall vanish away." You get what he is saying here? He's saying not only is love the greatest of Faith, Hope and Love, he's saying the thing, the only thing that will cross over from here to Heaven with us is love!

Tongues will cease when we leave this earth. Prophecies and vision stay here or they shall fail and wisdom and knowledge, it shall all vanish away. Whereas Agape love is eternal. The only language we'll speak is the knowledge of heaven common to us all. We'll hold conversations with everyone in perfect harmony and clarity. So you see, love has to be the key ingredient. Get it?

"I pray that He would grant you, according to the riches of His glory, to be strengthened with might by his Spirit in the inner man; that Christ may dwell in your hearts by faith, that ye, being rooted and grounded in love, may be able to comprehend with all saints what is the breadth, and length, and depth, and height; and to know the love of Christ, which passeth knowledge, that ye might be filled with all the fullness of God" (Ephesians 3:16-19).

God made us all each and every one of us to be His. His family, His sons and His daughters if you will. He wants us to act like that, like His sons and daughters, depending on Him, leaning on Him, needing Him, wanting Him, trusting and loving Him and to let Him love us. To trust and reach out to Him when we need to and also, I believe we need to chill out on the formal approach to God. We need to proceed like "kicking it with a friend." He wants to have a personal loving relationship with each and every one of us. We need to have a personal relationship with Him.

LOVE, NOT SPIKES HELD JESUS TO THE CROSS

You have to make a wish
Before it can come true
You have to dream a dream
Before a dream can work for you
For you to gain an inch
You first must walk a mile
For you to gain a friend
You first must learn to smile
There is an ancient law
As simple as can be
You have to know the truth
Before the truth can set you free.

Author: Joy Lovelet Crawford
Some wording modified by Frank

He Died For Me

"Love is the key that unlocks the bars of impossibility."

Fikayo Ositelu

Most of us interpret John 3:16 in different ways that are extreme or too broad or just plain out there bad in our thinking.

"For God so loved the world that He gave His only begotten Son, that whosoever believes in Him should not perish but have everlasting life" (John 3:16).

Yes, I know Jesus died for all the world but that's not what He did at all. I believe He died for me, as He died for you. Each and every one of us, not just a mass of people in the world. Me and you. If it were just me or just you in this whole world, He would have died for just me, or He would have died for just you. Wow. He would have gone through all of it, the human pain and suffering to feel and deal with all the sins, all the pain of the sins of the world. Incredible! Can you just imagine this?

Think about this for a moment. Think about how long it takes us, when we do something seriously wrong or when someone seriously hurts you. Look how painful one act may be and how long it might have taken us to deal with it and feel the pain. Sometimes we never get over it, right? Now however, Jesus dealt with and felt the pain of all mankind's sins. All of it. This type of sacrifice, suffering for one sole purpose. He endured it all, for me, for you, because He loved us so much. And it's always and forever and ever.

"He loves you with an everlasting love" (Jeremiah 31:3).

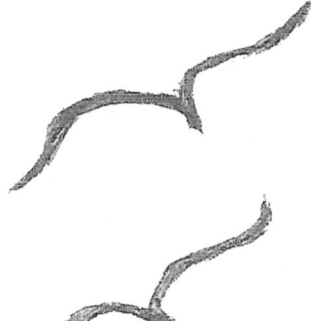

Book 3

We're All Special, Even Though

Even though we fall short, backslide and sin, through it all God says we are special. The devil will (and does) keep reminding us of our shortcomings. I know he hits me between the eyes all the time with them. My past mistakes continue to haunt me even right now. We need to be careful of certain things in our lives and in our pasts that can hold us down or keep us sick, or enable us to do things perhaps we would not normally do. In my life, I would hold on to some guilt or shame for something I did in the past, something stupid for example to get some money to buy dope. Then the devil would keep this crap in your face so you feel horrible (emotions) that you didn't make amends, that you didn't forgive yourself, that you committed the crime in the first place. You don't think God feels you're good enough or that He forgives you. So you stay sick longer. Beware of this sh*t as well.

In my life unfair, unjust, bogus sh*t happened many time in my past and I am constantly reminded by others of my past mistakes. This has caused me a lot of hurt, drama, pain and confusion that I am still dealing with today. Beware of the "what-ifs," the "should-be's" the "could-be's," the "if-only's," and the "why-me's." The world is unforgiving and our past comes back to hurt us. Some unfair, unjust things happen and the wounds and pain take, in some cases, many years to get over. Some of it you may never get over.

Watch out for this. I spent years remaining sick and not stepping through it because of self-pity with a bitterness and resentments. Why has it all happened to me? Where is this God? Why is there no help? Why didn't God help me? Anyway so dig this ok? It is life on life's terms. Simply that God always has a plan and reasons for all. Let it go and trust that. I had to let it go or die from drugs. Later, I realized I was the one causing the extra pain making myself miserable and worst of all, I was letting the devil slow down my progress and God's progress. I was wasting my time now, trying to make sense out of the past of yesterdays. For what? My life has not been all bad, however, and there is a flipside to this. So I must also share this with you. Many times when everything is going well, extremely well, all's good, you can't lose, nothing fails, and it's like gloating or drowning. In your wins or your victories, past and present, understand even that can keep you sick, and stop the progress you and God are making. The past is just that, the past. Don't use it against yourself.

And don't you let the devil use it against you either. No more! Whether victory or defeat it is over. Let's make a deal. I'll move on if you will. Deal? Deal! Cool.

Special – Valuable – Precious and LOVED

Do you know that God wants all of us to not only be special but feel special, not only be valuable, but to feel valuable, not only be loved, but feel loved? All of us, even those who have been hardened by life or by life circumstances, have deep within us a longing in our heart for love. God has truly made us all like this. Still there are way too many of us that can't believe God loves us each as individuals personally. We know God loves the world and we know God loves Jesus. Yet the Bible teaches that God loves us as much as He loves Jesus and that God loves us as much as He loves the world.

"The Father clearly loves the Son and discloses to Him everything that He Himself does, and He will disclose to Him greater things yet than these, so that you may marvel and be full of wonder and astonishment" (John 5:20). So first this says (now, check this out here okay?) God wants to thrill us, impress us, and amaze us by doing these great things for our pleasure and enjoyment. But now (dig this) this is what a lot of people miss. God wants to do not only for us, but even and especially through us. He wants us to look at the greatness of Jesus, at His great works He did through Jesus and then believe that He desires to do even bigger, better and greater things through "us."

Now listen to what Jesus said. "Verily, verily, I say unto you. He that believeth in Me, the works that I do shall he do also; and greater than these shall he do because I go unto my Father" (John 14:12).

"Know therefore that the Lord thy God. He is God the faithful who keepeth the covenant and mercy with them that love Him and keep His commandments to a thousand generations" (Deuteronomy 7:9).

Understand this everyone. His love for us is now and forever and ever and ever. It's also unconditional, meaning as bad as we are, as we backslide over and over, as we even repeat the same stupid mistakes over and over. We think and the devil would like us to think that God's tired of our crap. Right? Wrong! God can't be tired of us and we can't make Him stop loving us either. Understand this, love is not something God does. It's what and who He is. God is love. There isn't anyone or anything too bad for God to love. There's nothing He can't help us with. He has a plan, for you, for me, for all of us. For our restorations. He forgives our sins if we honestly and sincerely ask Him to. He also forgets them and "removes them as far as the East is from the West" (Psalm 103:10-14).

We might be saved. We might have received Jesus in our hearts and in our own ways even love Him. I know I truly do and you probably do to, but how much do we truly believe God loves us? This my friend is a very simple message. Yet it is also the most important and the very foundation of our lives and that is the everlasting unconditional love of God. This is what we all need to completely understand and focus on.

God gave man dominion and told us to "use all of the earth's resources in the service of God and man" (Genesis 1).

Consider this. Many Christians think we are to walk around miserable or poor as we help others. They think people can't be of means, having wealth and be of good as well. I don't think this is what God says in the Bible at all. It says He wants us to enjoy the whole world and to do so more abundantly. That sounds like He made it all for us, and it's all for us to enjoy. Not part of it, some of it, but all of it. Amen! "Then I realized that it is good and proper for a man to eat and drink, and to find some satisfaction in his toilsome labor under the sun during the few days of life God has given him for this is his lot. Moreover, when God gives any man wealth and possessions and enables him to enjoy them, this is a gift of God" (Ecclesiastes 5:18-19).

Do you realize that God does stuff for all of us every single day just because He loves us and somehow we never see it? This world is beautiful. Look at all the thought that went into it. The varieties of flowers that He gave us for instance. The fish in the sea, the animals and the wondrous oceans. For us. The sun in the sky, rain to help bloom and blossom and feed. For us. The beauty of snow on a tree branch. All from God for us. The smell of freshly cut grass, the different colors of the sky, the different shapes of the clouds. The list is endless and words cannot describe its majesty. And in all this He was and continues to look out for us, as He planned the perfect harmony of this our world. He has planned each and every one of our steps, so feel this!

CROSSROADS

We have come to a crossroads you and I
And I/We must either leave (or come with you) and you with "us"
Now and forever – forever,
I lingered, we linger over the choices long enough
But in the darkness of our doubts
You lifted the lamp of love
And I saw in your face and now you've seen in mine
The truth of our love
And the road we should take together
Today, tomorrow and through eternity.

Author: Frank

Co-Dependence as a Good Thing

Living in Dependence.

A big lie or a deceitful move with our thoughts is that the devil tries to make us compare and focus on the size or amount of our faith, rather than realize the real truth is that we should be more focused on the bigness of God.

GOD is the tree.

We are the branches.

The branch does not produce the fruit. It bears the fruit!

Remember in earlier chapters, I said God is the initiator of all. We are just the responders. God is the Creator and initiator of any and all things.

Jesus gives many examples of this co-dependence.

"I do nothing unless the Father tells me to do it. I tell you the truth the son can do nothing by Himself" (John 5:19).

"By myself I can do nothing. I judge only as I hear, and my judgment is just, for I seek not to please myself, but Him who sent me" (John 5:30).

"I say nothing unless the Father tells me to say it" (John 12:50).

"For I did not speak of my own accord, but the Father who sent me commanded me what to say and how to say it" (John 12:49).

So Jesus said, "When you lifted up the son of Man then you will know that I am the one I claim to be and that I do nothing on my own but speak just what the Father has taught me" (John 8:28).

"Don't you believe that I am in the Father and that the Father is in Me? The words I say to you are not just my own rather, it is the Father, living in me, who is doing His work. Believe me when I say that I am the Father and the Father is in me, or at least believe on the evidence of the miracle's themselves" (John 14:10-11).

The Love of God!

"And I pray that you being rooted and established in Love may have power together with all the saints, to grasp how wide and how long and deep is the Love of Christ and to know this Love that surpasses knowledge – that you may be filled to the measure of all the fullness of God" (Ephesians 3:17-20).

Wow. These guys sure wrote a lot better than I'll ever be able to. But you see my point here, right?

Bottom line here again. It's not even about us. It's all about God and His love for us. This love compelled and controlled Jesus. And as He was and is our greatest example of how we should be, feel and act, I believe that whatever we're dependent on for our meaning and purpose in our life these things will control you. Let me say this again. Whatever we're dependent on for our meaning and purpose in our lives these things will control you. Important note here, now dig this. Mankind was created by God to live in dependence upon his Creator (God) but not independent from Him. Whenever we refuse (and it's our choice, we choose here) to live in dependence upon "Christ" and God we are then forced to depend on Satan and the things of this world for our meaning and purpose to life. Crack cocaine, alcohol, any drugs, job, success, money, social status, popularity – these things will take you over. So I say the question is what are you controlled by? And what should we be controlled by? You guessed it. God's Love. "As the Father has loved me, so have I loved you. Now remain in my love" (John 15:9).

EXTERNAL FARTS IN OUR HEAD

I developed this diagram when facilitating the LifeLine Program in Whiteville, Tennessee, 1998. Actually, it's a continuum I got in early recovery. I believe it was from "Hazeldon's." However, I expanded it and took it a bit further and deeper.

Hazeldon's: Thoughts ⟶ feelings ⟶ actions

Thoughts lead to feelings. Feelings lead to actions.

Mine: Beliefs ⟶ values ⟶ thoughts ⟶ feelings ⟶ emotions ⟶ behaviors ⟶ actions ⟶ results ⟶ consequences

Beliefs lead to values. Values lead to thoughts. Thoughts lead to feelings. Feelings lead to emotions. Emotions lead to behaviors. Behaviors lead to actions. Actions lead to results. Results lead to consequences.

I developed this and present it here to show all we have to go through to act on one single thought. According to Jo-Ann Downey, author of Mental Clarity & Calmness, we average about 36,000 thoughts per day. Many years ago, I read that women speak approximately 6000-8000 words per day and men speak approximately 2000-4000 words per day. Dr. John Gray wrote a wonderful book called Men are from Mars, Women are from Venus about communications between the sexes. With her book, The Female Mind, Dr. Luan Brizendine found in her 2017 research that women speak 20,000 words per day compared to 7000 by men. She found that women devote more brain cells than men to speaking and that the simple act of talking triggers a rush of brain chemicals that give women a rush similar to that felt by heroin addicts when they get a high. But that's another matter. Thoughts are what I'm trying to talk about here. We all have thoughts, some good, some bad, some sinful and some beautiful. Nothing we can do about it.

First, what triggers these many thoughts?

The devil is the best at using your own self-talk against yourself. Remember when we said earlier the devil will torment you with thoughts about how bad you are. "Oh boy watch out, you screwed up now. You've done it now. Who do you think you are? God doesn't need you. God won't use someone like you. You broke the law, many laws as a matter of fact, you're no good."

This is a little something I got pertaining to the laws of man and even the laws of the Old Testament. Dig this: If a law had been given which was able to impart life, then righteousness would indeed have been based on these laws! Right. Yet, as is shown in this book and so many before it (a) we teach what we most need to learn, and (b) you and I can give from the learning and knowledge we receive from experiences (our great teacher vs. experiences).

However, my point here is simple. There is no law that can earn us favor or give life because law, any law is always connected to us and our own efforts, and our own efforts cannot give life. Jesus is the life, ok? Laws only condemn us and show our many sins, and proves overwhelmingly we need God and Jesus badly! Now back to those thoughts. Consider the learned beliefs and thoughts from parents, "You're a failure," or "You'll never amount to anything," or thoughts cemented into your head by a bad counselor, social worker, or wayward priest.

In the state where I live once you break the law you're doomed for life. It is the most unforgiving system in corrections, and clearly designed to fail. For example, they have a "forfeiture law" in my state. Let's say you're on parole after serving the confinement portion of your sentence. You're given a sentence of five years of confinement followed by six years of supervision. After you do your time and are out doing well, you can go all the way to your six year mark on supervision, get a parole officer mad at you, for whatever reason (like an ex-girlfriend calling and lying about you) and they will take away all the street time, the six years and make you start it over again. So virtually it can take you 40 years to complete one sentence for a crime (thought instilled by a system and backed by a parole officer). That is crowded, confused and corrupt. "You're an ex-con. You're a criminal. You're scum. Who will hire you? You've got a record. You don't deserve to live a good life." Then all those, and the other thoughts mentioned earlier, along with their prejudices, values and beliefs come into play and there you have it. Pure BS. I have points I want to make here. One is the bottom line and this is my warning to try to help those within the systems I mentioned earlier.

The devil has people so blinded that they'll die actually believing they are on the side of good. Like those in my state's correctional system. You can ask any parole or correctional officer and they will tell you that they are right and on the side of good. Note the bottom line. Law vs. grace. I said law vs. grace. Law and grace will not and cannot flow together. They are not even on the same page, and are impossible to be compatible. Even on the surface the appearance is clear why so many are fooled. On its surface law is or appears to be sensible in its appearance but guess what? The truth is it equals death guaranteed. The other grace, God's grace, appears to be absurd or crazy in its appearance, but it is life!

Been There, Done That

I had a revelation as I was writing this chapter. I realized I need to thank God for all the people I referred to on these pages that negatively affected my thoughts especially after now seeing the truth and experiencing people like the parole officer in my state. I have never seen a stricter, more legalistic bunch of lunatic, moronic, corrupt principle-keeping, dying-on-the-vine group in my life, and I've been a lot of places and have seen a lot of things. So get this, in experiencing these types of people I should thank God because now I never have to go back into that crap again. Now, there can't be anybody that's going to get me to go back to where they all are; trying to prove myself, back under the law, trying to please everyone even God by myself, efforts, words, or good deeds. This is a solid revelation here. Thank God because of these negatives in our lives and how we measure it from the time we trusted Jesus with a little faith to today, now trusting Jesus as our life. All the negative stuff that happened in between this time was for the purpose of bringing us back completely and fully to God's love, and this place, once truly experienced will leave you unable to possibly try anything else. Been there, done that, don't need to go back. Beware of the external motivations in your life as the thought continuum shows all we must go through before we act and respond to negative thoughts. It's a good tool I use and so can you to pause or take the time to decide what the thought is, where it comes from, and where it leads you. Time not to have responded negatively even if the thoughts are evil, negative, intentionally or not!

Internal vs. External Motivation

We can determine what our motivations are on all things we do before we do it. Are we motivated by things outside of us (external) or by the things within us (internal)? Here's a simple example. When I wanted to stop getting high on drugs, my mother asked me "to please stop." I tried. It didn't work. My employer sent me to a drug program once. I did the program. It didn't work. A parole officer once told me to do a program or I would go back to prison. Guess what? It didn't work. Why? Because these are all examples of external motivations. Also, note here that external things are usually of the world and this also is why they most likely won't last, and won't be good for us in the long run. Remember the only thing that we can take with us from this earth to eternity; the only thing we can carry over is the internal feelings within our hearts (of God), the stuff that truly counts. Long lasting, fulfilling, joyful, peace from within us from God and His love. The only thing we carry over is love.

Remember and please understand the type of person and the kind of mindset I had was all triggered from external experiences. I decided at the age of about 17 years old (based on my life experiences from about 7 – 17), that I could not trust love. I could not depend on anyone. Being independent, caring for no one was especially safe. With my feelings well-guarded, even when I was an entertainer, I learned not to get too close to any women in relationships I had. I would only go so far then I would run, run, run. I thought I had it all figured out that the least amount of help I had to ask for, the less I would attach myself to anyone emotionally. The less I attached true emotions to anything or anyone the less I could be hurt again. I thought this combined with getting high on drugs protected me from pain. I was, of course, very wrong. It took me what seems like forever to admit this and even longer to realize it and even longer to do something different about it. I spent far too many years in fear, worrying, upset, and angry over and over and over again. So understand why I said earlier in this book that the smarter we are (and it all starts with our thoughts, don't forget), and the more independent we become, the harder it is to believe and trust anyone else. Even God.

Opening a Can of Worms

Is knowledge power or what? Let me tell you another little quick story about me. When I got out of jail, I went into the car business. A friend of mine was the manager and helped me get in. Now get this, I didn't know one thing about cars. When I started I was the kind of guy that did not know how to change the oil and if I had a flat tire, I would sit there in the car, smoke a joint and call AAA to come fix it. To make a long story short, I was the top salesperson in the entire Chrysler zone for one year straight starting from my first day on the job. For one year straight I sold more cars than anyone from Milwaukee to Detroit. Remember, I didn't even know how to put oil in a car, but I sold more cars than anyone. So my friend, who was also the boss, became an owner of two dealerships. After my cocky butt asked him about management positions, he suggested I give him five years and my name would be on the sign out front. Back then five years to me was an outlandish length of time. He also suggested that if I learned about the product I would sell more cars. My reasoning, my way of thinking (arrogance, self-reliance) was to look at the sales board that showed I was so far on top I could not be caught by any of the old car snakes working there. I said, "Really, do all these guys know the product?" My friend and boss said, "Knowledge is power." I believed that for a long time. However, when to use it is another story.

Is knowledge power or can it keep you sick longer? Remember I said my intellectualizing kept me sick a lot longer than I needed to be. Well, I believe that. I get what my friend means because in the worldly sense of life the more you know about something the more confident you will be about it and the situation you're in. Like when I was selling cars. By the way, I did learn a little about the product along the way and went on to teach others how to sell cars.

Product knowledge in cars would tell you that for example, the Chevy Impala is available with six different size engines from 6 Cylinder to SS V8 power. So although I'm more confident in a discussion about this car in thought, is it something I should tell the customers? Why? If I have a car on the lot I want to sell why would I tell the customer this car comes with six different size motors when I'm trying to sell the one I've got, right? If he asks how strong the motor is, I say, "Let's take it for a ride and see if it is powerful enough for your needs." Why open up a can of worms about all the other engines? He might want to try them all before he buys. So again, you can see here how knowledge could indeed hamper you or slow you down, or even take you out, altogether, if you're not careful. And this is extremely true in what we're talking about in this book, isn't it?

If we rely on our own understanding, even in using the tools of this book and others, the more self-confident and self-righteous we become. This allows the devil in to tempt us. We don't have to let him in. We will never be delivered from reasoning, confusions, our negative thoughts, external motivation or our own false righteousness through our thinking and knowledge; it mostly all comes down to this, and that is faith.

"Faith is being sure of what we hope for and certain of what we do not see" (Hebrews 11:1). Faith is saying, "This I believe." It's saying, "I don't have to understand everything. I know the One who does." So I want to know the One who does better, instead of trying to figure out what He's up to. How do we know when we're getting better at this? When we start to worry less, fear less and have a lot less anxiety about everything in our lives. We talked about the devil using our past mistakes, through our self-talk, to hold us down or apart from God. Using others, even friends, parents, people in positions of power, all affect our thoughts leading to our behaviors and ultimate consequences. Remember and know this. God's love. He is the One who was, who is and who is still to come! So forgive yourself and others of the past no matter what. Because He was there before the foundation of the world. He knew you before you were born. Not only was He there at the beginning, He is the beginning. The Alpha. "I am the Alpha and the Omega," says the Lord God, "who is and who was and who is to come, the Almighty" (Revelation 1:8).

So now do you think He started the world and all of us for nothing? Don't worry about tomorrow! Does He get things going, then drop out? No, He will indeed finish what He's started for sure! He will be there in the end. He is the End. The Omega.

So it only goes to reason that He's got everything covered in between.

Please remember and know this in the midst of all the things in between the beginning (Alpha) and the end (Omega) I know how easy it is to let the devil get into your thoughts. I made the same mistakes over and over again because I allowed myself to feel guilty about those things I had done wrong. Those thoughts, which were evil, misguided thoughts, led to feelings of condemnation. Now remember and truly believe it is not by any works I can do, but by the love of God that forgives me for my mistakes and wrongdoings. This helps me now and will help you to stop doing the stupid stuff. Remember practice until it becomes a habit. Practice this. It will become automatic and then watch out! Fear, guilt, anger, resentment and shame keeps us all weighed down and extremely depressed and even makes us want to give up at times, right? It weighs us down to the point we can't even be free, thus making us feel helpless and powerless to the point we're falling back into the same old crap, and sins appear easier and we repeat the stupid behavior. STOP IT! I said STOP IT. Be cool and dig this. We must begin to operate more in faith. Stop and refuse to stay stuck in fear, guilt, anger, resentment and shame, all of it! Don't forget the devil in all its many disguises will come at you and say, "You got to feel like sh*t about that one buddy. That was a bad one you did again this time." All we have to say is, "No, I'm not. No, I'm not stuck. No, I'm not helpless. No, I'm not powerless, not at all." Remember it's hard to do it and believe it at first but also remember the more you do it, practice it, you'll see. Trust me. It gets easier and then it will become automatic.

This following scripture explains it even better than I ever could.

"Surely He took up our infirmities and carried our sorrows, yet we considered him stricken by God, smitten by Him, and afflicted. But he was pierced for our transgressions, He was crushed for our iniquities. The punishment that brought us peace was upon Him and by His wounds, we are healed" (Isaiah 53:4-7).

So when Jesus took our sins for us, He also took away the guilt of sin (and that includes all the crap that goes along with it, like the feelings). The devil, however, doesn't want us to be free of this because if or when he has us in the negative thought pattern of guilt, we cannot truly get as deep as we should into the love of God. This will separate us and we can't truly appreciate or enjoy His presence as intended. Why? Because the devil takes the focus off of God and puts it on "us." Get it? So let's walk free. People, walk free from this guilt, from this fear, from this shame and believe it when God said His grace was sufficient to cover all your sins. His grace and forgiveness are gifts. He meant it all and He loves me and He loves you.

God's Pipeline

GOD'S PIPELINE

Water can flow through it at will, nothing to block, clog or slow it down.
Nothing can stop this positive flow.

Our pipeline blocks God's plan with all our BS not only slowing down His plans and processes for our growth and others as well, but even stopping and causing long delays. "Come to me, all ye who labor and are heavy laden, and I will give you rest" (Matthew 11:28).

Whatever causes our fear and stress, our hurt and our pain in fact is preventing the flow of God's pipeline. The heart of God is the place to leave these emotions. Leave it all with Him for He cares for you and nothing can overcome Him. You see, I believe our Bible that God gave us holds any and all the answers we need. We just need a little help seeing it there at times. The Bible is like our guidebook from God to us. "All scripture is given by inspiration of God, and is profitable for doctrine, for reproof, for correction, for instruction in righteousness" (2 Timothy 3:16).

The apostle Paul also tells us many things and this he says a lot, "That God has a heart of love for us."

"Who shall separate us from the love of Christ? Shall trouble or hardship or persecution or famine or nakedness or danger or sword? No, in all these things we are more than conquerors through Him who loved us. For I am convinced that neither death nor life, neither angels nor demons, neither the present nor the future, nor any powers, neither height nor depth, nor anything else in creation, will be able to separate us from the love of God that is in Christ Jesus our Lord" (Romans 8:35-39).

"If God is for us, who can be against us?" (Romans 8:31) Does this cover the point here or not?

You know I'm not sure exactly where I heard this or maybe I read it somewhere but it stuck with me and it seems to fit here as well. It's that life is not made by the dreams we have but by the choices we make.

Acceptance. Accountability. Responsibility.

These three words used together are a great tool.

Our lives today are the exact total of all the choices we have made up to now.

Remember these three words in life and remember the thought continuum from the previous chapters. We always have time from our thoughts to the actual choices we make. Plenty of choices and don't forget, plenty of time between the thought and the actions or behavior of it. However, we always seem to end up with an assortment of these choices. You would think that our choices would be better knowing all this information, right? Wrong. Like all of us, the choices I've made have ranged from really bad to sometimes excellent.

God wants us to move across the continuum I'm talking so much about, past all our BS, like in the Lifeline or all our BS in the pipeline of our poor choices (be them natural impulses or not). All the way past all these life lessons to all the excellent choices. That's what God wants! And it stands to reason it should be what we want as well. However, I know, believe me I know, that often it's a real challenge to make these excellent choices especially living life on life's terms when we're standing all alone or our options are few and far between. Remember Shadrach, Meshach and Abednego, the three men who were facing a fiery death? What were their choices? Deny Jesus or burn?

There was a situation in my life and this is a very good example of how God moves so we can learn and grow from it. I was in jail and I had a pending charge hanging over my head as well. I had to serve 13 months and 17 days, with the threat of getting a lot more time for the new charge. The prosecution even had the alleged co-defendant set to testify as to my alleged involvement in this crime. Now also understand I had a very well-paid lawyer representing me, who was pathetic and disliked by court staff. The District Attorney had him bamboozled and intimidated, although he never would admit that. She told him I was done, a goner. Going to the penitentiary, no doubt about it. If I didn't take a deal I would go away for even longer. And she would hit me with many charges. She said she had the co-defendant to rat on me (or lie "really" for her own deal) and I better plead to the new charge or else. My lawyer swore up and down, "She has you by the balls. Take the deal, plead and take your chances with the Judge or it's going to be a lot worse. We can't win." So anyway, to make a long story short here, I did my 13 months, 17 days, and got released on bail on the new charge. I went to court all by myself from the outside. I saw my "great" lawyer. He once again tried his hardest to get me to plead guilty and beg for mercy. The District Attorney was there, feeling pretty smug just knowing that my lawyer was going to talk me into taking that deal. At this time, I was living deep in sin, high on drugs, sex outside of marriage, and other things I'm not proud of. I walked into court with my suit on, still glassy-eyed from being up the night before on cocaine and the District Attorney said to my lawyer in front of the Judge, "Well, well, are we ready to get this over with? Is your client ready to plead out today?" My lawyer looked at me one last time. By the way, and this is important, all year I was getting what I believe were messages from God. The latest messages were to take a stand on this matter, to trust God and stand.

Now I don't need to tell you the fear I felt. I've been to jail a lot before. I know how the system works and I was scared I was going to get railroaded on my bad record alone. As happens often in my state, the District Attorney was determined to get me bad and also threatened my lawyer that if I didn't plead she would hit me heavy and hard with many more charges, higher bails and I would go away forever, ok. So my lawyer looked at me and said, "Deal or no deal." I said, "No deal, let's go to trial." My lawyer looked at the District Attorney weakly, shaking his head and said, "No deal. He doesn't want any deals. Period!" The judge looked up, remembering the District Attorney's threats from the last hearing, and the DA said, "The State dismisses the charge." That's right, the State dismissed the charge, and then she said, "The State would like to reserve the right to bring up this charge at a later time." The Judge dismissed the charges against me and returned all the bail money as well. The DA, of course, was extremely mad. She threatened me again and told my lawyer she would be charging me with a lot of stuff and that the bail was going to be so high I would not get out next time. However, to date there have been no charges. Praise God.

You see, I did have a pretty good defense pending. One year on my own working on this matter, with the strong help and support of my girlfriend, but the point here is crystal clear to me. God showed me that when He's ready and the time is right, trust His timing, His will, His protection, His mercy, His power. Not mine! All the worry, stress, frustration, pain and anger was for nothing. All I had to do all along is trust in God. Listen to Him and "stand." Even in sin, and this is important because this shows there is nothing at all that we can do to earn favor or grace. Period! He did it because it was His time to show me this revelation and take me to the next level. We are powerless to earn or deserve God's grace, mercy and love. We get it when it's right and we get it just because God's God. The devil used it all against me on this one. All my doubts, all my fears, lack of faith, pride, anger, concerns about the system, fears about myself in sin, the guilt, shame, the District Attorney, the Judge, the lawyer, plenty of frustrations. The devil came with it all but yet and still God told me to stand, then wiped it all away. Amen. Praise God.

Always remember. The Bible is our guidebook. This tells us which road to take, when to travel, when to turn. Actually it tells us when we are off the road and tells us how to get onto the right road. Instruction in righteousness tells us how to stay on God's road. The mistakes and all the bad choices that lead us away from God's road are not to be taken in stride or lightly. We should learn, grow or move on, or God may repeat the lesson over and over until we get it. God is the best GPS device we will ever have.

But know this, most of our failures (well, all of them actually) are seldom fatal and very, very few are final, so get this. If it didn't kill you, then God is giving you yet another chance.

You can't be found unless you're lost. "For the Son of Man came to seek and to save what was lost" (Luke 19:40).

Make the choice to live a life filled with the stuff that keeps the pipe crystal clear so we can flow with the goal stuff like joy, peace, patience, kindness, goodness, faithfulness, gentleness, self-control and you all know the next one. LOVE. God's love. Then be ready to be triumphant in all things.

Book 4

Keep Doing What You Always Did – You'll Get What You Always Got

BETTER TOMORROW

I never knew there would be a better tomorrow,

But you've come into my life and taken away all my sorrow

My days of sadness are a thing of the past

Because I have found Love at last

My days of emptiness are gone for good,

Because you filled a void in my heart that you should

You've opened the window,

You've shown me the light

And my love for you will

Continue to burn bright.

Author: Yvonne Warren

When I was a little younger than I am now I walked a lot. I still walk as much as possible but back then I used to walk down this road called addiction and bondage. I walked down the road for many years, and it's funny because every time I walked down this same road I came to a big old hole right smack in the same place in the road every time. It's crazy I know, but I would just walk right up to the hole in the road and fall right down into it. Every time. I can't even tell how many times I did this.

Albert Einstein said, "Insanity is doing the same thing over and over again and expecting different results."

So after many years of falling and falling and falling into the same old hole in this same old road, you know what I finally did? I decided to take another road.

Really God Me?

"And hope does not disappoint us, because God has poured out His love into our hearts by the Holy Spirit, whom He has given us. You see, at just the right time, when we were still powerless, Christ died for the ungodly. Very rarely will anyone die for a righteous man, though for a good man someone might possibly dare to die. But God demonstrates His own love for us in this; while we were still sinners Christ died for us. Since we have now been justified by His blood, how much more shall we be saved from God's wrath through Him! For if, when we were God's enemies, we were reconciled to Him through the death of His Son, how much more, having been reconciled, shall we be saved through His life!" (Romans 5:5-10)

Wow, this scripture says it all.

Bottom line, I'm not and you're not good enough. Period! But the beauty of it all is we don't have to be. Jesus has been good enough in our place. He paid for our sins and took the punishment all of us deserved. Yes, all of us.

The Bible says that, "If He loves us enough to die for us, how much more than, being justified by His blood, does He love you?" (Romans 5:8-9)

The answer is simple. Clearly He loves us enough to keep us, and to cover our daily wrongs, bad choices and mistakes and keep us cleansed enough for all unrighteousness. This is what God does for us all. He is more than able to work it all out, everything big or small and in between for the good of all of us if we love Him. He can and will keep us all on the path of true progress if we continue to seek Him.

One time I was deep into my addiction, in the world on a long binge smoking cocaine. I was on a non-stop mission, up for many days and nights, hanging out with the prostitutes and the druggies partying with no end in sight and all that lifestyle entails. I remember this story because it really doesn't fit the norm of stories like this because most people don't call out for God's help unless they are in big trouble or they hit bottom, right? Well, here I was driving around getting everybody and their baby brothers and sisters high for weeks on end. I finally was alone, driving my brand new Park Avenue Ultra on the south side of town. I had over $5000 cash in my pocket and a bunch of cocaine to boot. So I was by no means down and out but I knew I was dying in sin and in deep, deep trouble as it hit me all at once. What was I doing? Did I want to kill myself or what? So all of a sudden I pulled to a stop in the middle of the road. I just pulled to a stop in the middle of Greenfield Avenue, an extremely busy street. I got out, got on my knees right in the middle of the road and cried out, "God help me!" I cried for a moment crying out for God's help, got back into the car, turned off the busy street because I couldn't see with all the tears in my eyes, and not more than 100 feet from that turn, I was four-pointed by police cars—at least eight to nine cars. Where did they all come from so fast? Impossible right? They arrested me, found the cocaine, seized my car and money, and the party was over. Just like that. I believe I was saved that day in the middle of the road and God's been working on me since.

You see, this is something to get extremely excited about as I attempt to put all the pieces of my life's puzzle together. "For thou art a holy people unto the Lord, thy God. The Lord thy God had chosen thee to be a special people unto Himself, above all people that are upon the face of the earth. The Lord did not set His love upon you, nor choose you because ye were more in number than any people; for ye were the fewest of all people" (Deuteronomy 7:6-7).

GOD HAS NOT PROMISED

God has not promised skies always blue,
Flower-strewn pathways all our life through
God has not promised sun without rain,
Joy without sorrow, peace without pain.
But God has promised strength for the day.
Rest for the labor, light for the way
Grace for the trails, help from above
Unfailing sympathy, undying love.

> *Verse 1 and 2 Hymn*
> *Written by Annie Johnson*

Love God Back!

I don't think many of us at all know very much about loving God. We can barely love one another much less even ourselves right? You see, as you all well know by now, God doesn't always seem to answer as fast as He did when I was high on the street. In fact, sometimes God doesn't even seem to care, or God never seems to even answer. He doesn't seem to even hear us at times, right? Have you been there in that thinking? I know you have. Me too. Here's what I believe this shows us at least in part.

Do you suppose (now feel me on this) that God just wants us to love Him the way He loves us? In a lot of our prayers and as I said in previous chapters, we love or know how to love conditionally, right? The kind of love we get something in return for, and there is and always will be a lot of this kind of love out there in the world. This is even taught in religion and even in some Christian faith groups. Our sinful "fleshy love" will always be like this and (follow me on this) even when I was growing or thought I was becoming a deeper Christian, I still was looking for a reward, something conditional for my Christian efforts. Know what I mean? First from love between a man and a woman – I love you because what you do for me. Then even with God – I love you because you have blessed me or given me this and that. Bottom line? The flesh always wants a reward. Again, I ask is this not a good reason for God at times to make us wait to answer our prayers. Is it that God wants us to love Him and others the same way He loves us?

We were loved before any of us even thought about or even attempted to turn to God. God loved us and He didn't get anything back at all then. And He wasn't getting anything back when we as humans fell. He was and always is just loving. Only loving.

Just think a minute. Do you think that some of the pain that we all go through, when we don't seem to get anything from God, is all just part of the process to understand the real love we're supposed to give? So that we'll now be able to love Him with that special love. This would in fact then be God's love starting to love Him back. Us loving God the way God loves us? Up to now you and I wanted to love God if He would perhaps bless us with something, nice homes, good health, save our kids from pain, keep our cars and toys. We love Him, but we think He ought to be doing something for us.

But there is a deeper level, a far better level of understanding here. A level that will change your life. I guarantee it. A deep eternal knowledge that we just fall in love with God because He's God. We love God in the same way He loves us. He didn't have to learn to do it. He can't help it, so also then we can't help but love Him. I know and I believe it's hard for many of us to believe that God's main objective would be that we just love Him. It's true! However, at times I believed that God wanted me to save the world, and to just love God seems like a half measure to a worldly objective mind. Yet when we start reading all those psalms in the Bible and all the heavy expressions of love toward God from them what's the best way we can think of to get to know God better? What better way than to fall in love with God (without the rewards).

When we're in the early stages of our lives like little kids the emphasis is on what we do. It's on ourselves, right? But as we grow up it changes to a more mature stage with the emphasis on the Father. "I write to you, fathers because you have known Him who is from the beginning. I write to you young men because you are strong and the word of God lives in you, and you have overcome the evil one" (1 John 2:14). You see our focus shifts finally from us to Him (the Father) or should eventually.

When we do then we'll experience the love of God at a new deeper level. We'll be more spirit and soul, satisfying experiences we could ever imagine possible.

Love is its own end. To love and be loved, that is the essence of the life we live. That is the essence of the kingdom to come. To love and be loved.

I WROTE YOUR NAME IN THE SKY

I wrote your name in the sky but the wind blew it away

I wrote Your name in the sand but the waves washed it away

I wrote Your name in my heart and forever it will stay.

Author: Jason Graham

Have Faith, Trust More, and Stop Complaining

"For in Christ Jesus neither circumcision nor uncircumcision has any value. The only thing that counts is faith expressing itself through love" (Galatians 5:6).

Here's what I think about faith. First it's not really something tangible that you have and I also believe it's a form of works. I think one of our biggest mistakes is that we spend way too much of our time trying to please everyone, especially the elders in our churches, but also we try to earn favor with God by doing well.

Now we know that without faith we cannot please God so we spend all our time and efforts trying to have more faith thinking God will then like us more. So do you suppose we can walk in faith if we think we're not good enough in God's sight or anyone else's?

"For we walk by faith, not by sight" (2 Corinthians 5:7).

So you see faith is of the heart as well. Energized and expressed and working through love. We get it only through our loving friendship with God. Faith is simply this: it's our hands trusting and reaching out so as we can and receive from God. Faith is leaning on God, trusting and being confident in Him. It's not something we can earn by doing good works.

Anyone who thinks he or she is not good enough in God's eyes will not walk in faith. Get it? Always know and remember we have been made right with God only through Jesus' sacrifice. Our being right with God is not based on what we have done, or will be in the future, or any of that. It is only based on what Jesus did. So any person who thinks they're not good enough or won't amount to anything, or feel they are pathetic failures and that God can't, won't or doesn't love them will not walk in faith.

Also, stop complaining. I stayed sick with it a long time because of my bitching and constant comparing and complaining. I would think and say things like, "Life's not fair. Why me Lord? How come they get all the breaks? Why do I always get treated unfairly?" I can give you example after example to fit these and even be justified in some of it but I won't give you story after story. What I will say is that it makes no sense to bitch or complain because it doesn't fix anything. Instead it wastes good time you could spend on being positive or correcting something else. It also opens the door for the devil to come in and do his thing like take our joy away for the moment or our peace. Remember I talked earlier about external motivations? Trying to control things outside of us is a waste of time. We cannot control people, places and things. All we can do is control how we respond to them. The minute we try to control them we put forth expectations, and all the other issues we have become involved like trust. We then have set ourselves up for failure and we let the devil in. How do we know if we're operating externally vs. internally? By knowing things like peace, joy, mercy are from the inside of us. Things like fear, dread, confusion, frustration are all external. Get it? Note here, if we stay full of the right stuff and we do this by keeping all our thought on this new found love friendship with God, the devil's attempts to steal our joy and peace through misguided thoughts will have no place or effect or meaning in us. "Do not be overcome by evil, but overcome evil with good" (Romans 12:21).

Here's a better example that is out of the Bible (I won't use another boring one out of my life). We probably all have heard of and seen the movie, *The Ten Commandments*, one of the greatest films I think ever made. Anyway we all know the story but what follows is something we may not have fully understood or thought about. Remember, "Have faith, trust more and stop complaining."

To enjoy all the inheritance God has for you, get in agreement with Him to receive all He wants to give! "And you also were included in Christ when you heard the word of truth, the gospel of your salvation. Having the promised Holy Spirit, who is a deposit guaranteeing our inheritance until the redemption of those who are God's possessions to the praise of His glory" (Ephesians 1:13-14).

In Deuteronomy 1:26-28 we learn the Israelites had bad attitudes toward everything. It says, "They were peevish and disconnected. They murmured, they complained." They all thought that possessing the Promised Land was a stretch, hard work and an effort. It was easier to not confront the total situation. They wanted everything to come to them easily. "But you were unwilling to go up; you rebelled against the command of the Lord your God. You grumbled in your tents and said, 'The Lord hates us so he brought us out of Egypt to deliver us into the hands of the Amorites to destroy us. Where can we go? Our brothers have made us lose heart. They say, the people are stronger and taller than we are; the cities are large, with walls up to the sky. We even saw the Anakites there'" (Deuteronomy

1:26-28). Been there, done that, right? I can't even begin to tell you how many times I ran from responsibilities for these same reasons. Anyway, remember that they were like this even though people were actually talking to God at this time. Going up on mountains and coming down with tablets with God's laws on them (The Ten Commandments). In spite of all the miracles they had the privilege of seeing, like the splitting of the Red Sea and Moses striking the rock so they could have water to drink still they did not trust enough. They did not have enough faith and they continued to complain. Therefore, the devil found his opening. The Israelites began to fear and did not trust Him to guide them, to protect and take them to the Promised Land. They listened to and trusted their fears instead.

Now dig this! It only takes about 11 days to get from Horeb the way they would have to go through Mount Seir to Kadesh Barnea which is on the Canaan's border. Yet, guess how long it took the Israelites to get there? Not 11 days. It took them 40 years to get there! 40 years instead of 11 days. Why? It was because of their complaining and lack of faith. So let's all learn and continue to be aware of what I'm talking about in this book that can slow us down and keep God from doing His will for us. We have to stop allowing the devil to get in. I know I have to. How about you? Let's keep stepping toward God asking Him to help us all recognize the issues we have that is destroying our growth. Replace our old minds with His new ones of His Truth, trust, faith and His love. Let's stop struggling so hard and spend our time instead with God as a true friend using our efforts to love Him and receive His love.

BELIEVE

What is there to believe in during life?

Nothing lasts aside from strife

Life may perish

Life may end

Our soul we may give

Our soul we may spend

But our love!

That eternal flame

Will never dim,

Will never change

It will last forever last,

When all other light leaves.

Author: Tyler Dohrn

Life Is All About It

"And so we know and rely on the love God has for us. God is love and he that lives in love lives in God, and God in him" (1 John 4:16).

Life is all about love. Life's meaning is to love because God is love and God created life. Pretty simple when you break it down, and believe it is in loving that we become as close to being like Jesus, our greatest example as to how and what we should be like. Like God. So love is the total key here. The beginning (the foundation) and through to the end of life on earth, and then through eternity. So now that we know this all important truth of what life is all about, it's time to prioritize a little, don't you think? I mean, didn't God tell us to? He not only tells us to. He gives us a lot of time to figure it out and learn how to do it better as well. 1 Corinthians 13:3 says, "If I give all I possess to the poor and surrender my body to the flames, but have not love, I gain nothing." In other words, no matter what I say, what I believe and what I do, I'm bankrupt without love.

Love means living the way God commands us to live. As you have heard from the beginning, His command is this: that we walk in love. "And this is love; that we walk in obedience to His commands. As you have heard from the beginning, His command is that you walk in love" (2 John 6).

It's becoming clearer yet, isn't it? How then can we tap into it? How can we become more in tune to God's love? Because no matter how much He loves us, if we are not plugged into it or aware of it, it can't or won't benefit us. You know how cool it feels when someone comes into your life and shows you affection, even a little love. Do you remember when you were in school and a new girlfriend would come around, smile and show some love toward you? Remember how this gave you confidence? Well, this must also be the truth with God as well, right? God loves us and He wants to show us that love. On a much higher level than the high school sweethearts, of course, but still the same formula must be in place. Now hold on, I'm just like you and I don't even come close to pretending I have all the answers, but this makes sense, right? I believe God does and has invited each and every one of us into a personal, caring and honest, loving relationship with Him. He wants in on everything we do. Just like an ongoing friendship back in school growing up where we would share and talk about everything and I mean everything with your closest and best friend.

Love is the Foundation of Life.

In addition to the commandments to Love Thy Neighbor and Love the Lord Your God with all your Heart, love is clearly the foundation of God's other commandments as well.

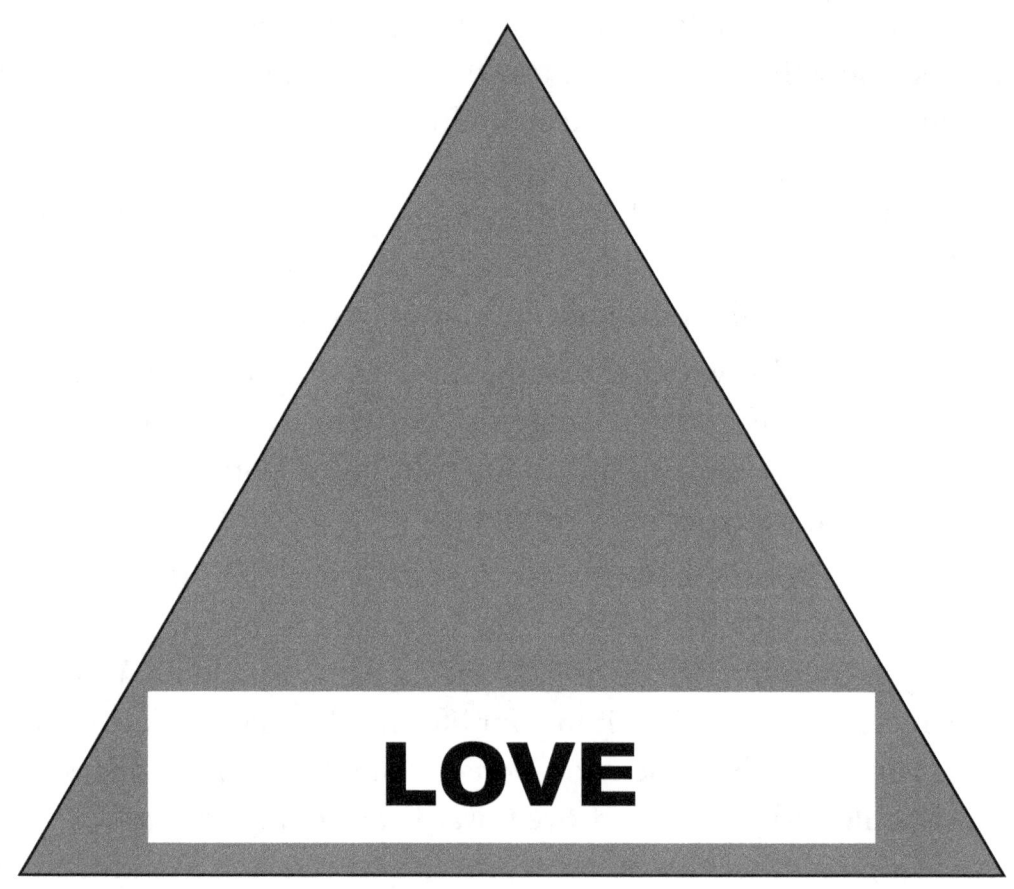

FOUNDATION OF LIFE!

Shouldn't Life Be to Just Love?

Love should, for all of us, be the most important thing in our lives. Without a doubt, right? Jesus said it. Peter said it. Paul said it. God commands it. So love should not be just a nice part of your life. Many of us seem to fit a love life into a schedule that includes careers and other time-consuming tasks, and it seems to be directly related to sex at the same time. Now how did that happen? Understand this, ok? Love per God and his disciples (saints all of them) make it clear love should not just be a part of your life. It should be, without a doubt, the most important part of your life. The Bible says in 1 Corinthians 14:1, "Let love be your greatest aim." So then why do we say stuff like "one of the things I want out of life is to find that one special person to love, but if I don't, oh well!" Or, "I want to be more loving to others." The point I'm trying to make here is that love is not something we're supposed to try to get to perhaps or eventually in life. It's supposed to be our Number One priority. Remember what Paul was saying in 1 Corinthians 13:3, that "Life without love is really worthless." Think about this people, please! I'm on to something here. Paul said as well, "No matter what I say, what I believe and what I do, I'm bankrupt without love."

Don't forget that Jesus Himself summed it all up. "You must love the Lord your God with all your heart and with all your soul, and with all thy mind, and with all thy strength. This is the first and greatest commandment." Second is equally important, "Love your neighbor as yourself."

So now we start learning to love God more and we better start learning to love others as well, right?

I believe when we truly start applying the love thing here, our busy schedule allows the enemy to combat this. Now pay attention. Most of us have to work at least ten hours per day to get by. Then we have to sleep at least 8-10 hours depending on how hard we work, leaving about four hours to travel, eat, clean, have fun, and spend on our love relationships. And note we must do this or we're probably not living an honest lifestyle, right? So who set up this unrealistic, rigid life-work schedule? Someone influenced the government to put this in place this way, right? Don't you think the devil knows that if we have to spend so many hours to just live and survive that we must begin to sacrifice what our loving God tells us is the most important thing in our lives for us to first learn and then do? We must stop being preoccupied with our work, making a living, paying off all our bills and setting, even reaching goals that we thought were so important in life because they're not! The point to life is learning to love God and people.

RECIPE FOR TWO LOVERS

Take happiness and laugher, mix thoroughly with romance
Add hugs, pecks and sprinkle it all with kisses
Bind with pleasure and bake with faith
Then serve with endless love.

Author: Jephthah Adotey

Book 5

Our Insides Cannot Change

Here is yet another point I believe is worth making in our seemingly endless list of solid truths about our newfound meaning of life. You know you can be imprisoned, punished for things you may or may not have done. You can be tortured and made to say whatever they want you to say, but here is a solid fact. There isn't anything anyone can do to make you change your mind or make you believe something that's not what you believe to be right. Something that goes against what you believe to be right, what you feel inside and in your heart. Circumstances can change your house, car, life, appearance, and your identity, all of it. But it can't change what's in your heart and what's in your heart is love. What's right and wrong is also decided within our hearts.

Here's an example of how the courts and society influences everything. In fact, society is trying in some very serious ways to get in the way of God's progress with us and vice versa. The gay rights issue is controversial, as well as the issue of abortion and the right to bear arms. In 1934 the Veterans of Foreign Wars (VFW) erected the Mojave Desert Veterans Memorial Cross on top of Sunrise Rock in the middle of the 1.6 million acre Mojave National Preserve in honor of fallen World War I veterans. In 2001 a single individual represented by the American Civil Liberties Union (ACLU) sued, saying it was unconstitutional to have the cross at that location since it was on government land. The lower courts agreed. A heavy bag was placed over the cross and it was padlocked. Later this was replaced by a wooden box. It remained covered during the appeals process. In 2010 the Supreme Court reversed the decision of the lower courts. A few days after the Supreme Court ruling, vandals stole the cross. In 2012 ownership of the land where the cross was located was transferred to the VFW. The cross was restored and rededicated. So you see, the symbol of the cross has and will probably always be controversial until the day of His return. Paul said, "For Christ did not send me to baptize, but to preach the gospel, not with words of human wisdom, lest the cross of Christ be emptied of its power" (Corinthians 1:17).

My point is the message of the cross means nothing and may seem goofy to those who don't believe it on the inside or in their hearts. But to those of us who believe in it on the inside or in our hearts it's the absolute power and grace and love of God. Paul further says in Corinthians 1:18, "For the message of the cross is foolishness to those who are perishing, but to us who are being saved it is the power of God." The devil in knowing or sensing this opportunity to block or prevent growth can easily intervene using our court system or our society's leaders or lawmakers. The cross, its meaning, and our true inner beliefs about it will be decided in our hearts, and this decision cannot be changed by anyone but us.

"I will give you a new heart and put a new spirit in you; I will remove from you your heart of stone and give you a heart of flesh" (Ezekiel 36:26).

And let's also not forget that this stuff on the inside I'm talking about is the only stuff on earth in our lives we take with us to eternity. Point being that love lasts forever. God tells us that love is eternal and to make it the Number One priority. These are the things on the inside I'm talking about. "These three things continue forever; Faith, Hope and Love and the greatest of these is Love" (1 Corinthians 13:13).

"What lies beneath us and what lies before us are tiny matters compared to what lies within us."

Ralph Waldo Emerson

A Very Common Denominator

LIFE – LOVE = ZERO

Truly realizing that God loves you gives a person a lot more confidence in themselves, as well as a lot more confidence and trust in God's faithfulness to us. All sorts of positive and truly fruitful blessings will come, has to come, once we accept God's love. Greater faith. Victory over sin. Peace in your heart. Healings. A life rich in His gifts, and we know that's endless, and joy. It all has to come by letting God love us. Let's not get it twisted here. We might lean toward and believe that "no, no, I have to love God." But this is important enough to say it over again. I think we have to let God love us first. I believe what it says in the Bible, "That we love Him, because He first loved us" (1 John 4:19).

IN LOVE

The day You appeared, I lost my heart to You, to love
And from that day I cannot part from You – from love
You hold me tight to You, to love
I offer all I have to give to You to love
And all my days I want to live with You, in love.

Author: Amanda Marie Burson

Love will also leave a legacy. It's the strongest impact on earth to date.

I want to bring up an important observation here because it is relevant to the issue at hand. You may remember in earlier chapters I talked about how much I read. I have learned a lot from the smartest biblical teachers, self-help scholars, psychologists, theologians, professors, doctors and more. I tried to read and learn it all. The list is long, and many, if not all of these people are much brighter than I'll ever be. Throughout their teachings, there are issues of debate, disagreement or controversy among them, but there is one concept they all seem to agree upon. This one concept is mentioned in all of their books, as well as in the Bible. They all agree in the power and importance of love. Some of these great authors give it a few pages, some give it more, but they all agree on its importance and feel the strong desire to write about it.

So my question is simple. Can all these experts and well-educated people be wrong? What I've done here is simply this. I've lined up this issue within this book and the concepts referred to with some of the best. I also lined it up with the people God anointed to write the Bible, and their teachings and brilliant words of wisdom. It's lined up with what Jesus Himself taught and said. And clearly lined up most importantly with God's teachings and commands, so it is safe to say and I'm very confident that I'm among some very excellent company when I say that "love" being the answer, our answer, to the question of "What's the Meaning of Life" is correct.

"Your greatness is not measured by how many people serve under you, but by how many people you serve."

John Hagee

And so we know and rely on the love God has for us. "God is love and whoever lives in love lives in God and God in him" (1 John 4:16).

"As the Father has loved me, so have I loved you."

(John 15:9)

"For in Him, we live and move and have our being as some of your own poets have said, 'we are His offspring'" (Acts 17:28).

So what they're saying is we need God for everything. For peace when in trouble, help in time of need, victory over temptation. We need Him for forgiveness, purpose, eternal life, and we need Him for love.

"May your love increase and overflow for each other and for everyone else just as ours does for you."

(1 Thessalonians 3:12)

God Didn't Gamble on You or Me

First, God's total purpose did in fact take into consideration everything so you better believe He knew and was aware of all our future human mistakes and errors to come – past, present and future. And yes, you better believe He knew all our sins were to follow us all as well. Nothing God does is by guessing, by mistake or by accident. You better believe He has an absolute reason for each and everything He created. All of it was planned by Him. The fish in the sea, all the plants, every animal, and abundantly more examples, and so it's clearly safe to say each and every person was planned with a purpose in God's mind. So please understand this. We can't possibly know all the purposes God still has planned for our future and through eternity but I am certain of one thing. I can guarantee to you what God's motive was for creating us. His motive for creating us was His love. The Bible says in Ephesians 1:4, "According as He hath chosen us in Him before the foundation of the world, that we should be holy and without blame before Him in love." In other words, long before He laid down earth's foundation, He had us in mind, and had settled on us as the focus of His love.

So God was thinking of me and you even before He created our world. In all fact and truth, it's why He created it! Why else? We were and still are since the beginning. Why? Because it's safe to say we are the focus of this great love of God and the most valuable of all his creations as well, right? The Bible also says, "God decided to give us life through the word of truth so we might be a kind of firstfruits of all He created" (James 1:18).

Remember I've said in earlier chapters that we should not worry so much. We're all fixable because we're created by a mastermind! Well, let me go on here. The deeper involved our great scientists and all the other experts in these fields get, one thing becomes ever clearer. God planned it all with great precision. The more we learn about our earth the more we cannot deny how all of it was uniquely designed for our specific existence. All custom made for us with specifications that can make only our human life even possible. Bottom line here is this. All the facts and evidence concludes and supports that our world, and all God created in it, was specifically designed with life and mankind as its main goal and fundamental purpose. Also the Bible said the same thing, "God formed the earth… He did not create it to be empty but formed it to be inhabited" (Isaiah 45:18). Why did God go through all this trouble of creating our world, a whole wide world for us? There can only be one answer. Because He loves us. Because He's a God of love. Obviously, this level of love is pretty hard to comprehend (for our level of understanding), but we can decipher its meaning when it comes to our existence. It's reliable to know that we were indeed created as a special important part of God's love. As special objects of God's love, so He could do one thing and that's love us. This is in my opinion absolute truth. All facts scientific and beyond prove it to be the truth. There is a perfect love and God made us all to express it. Now that's something to build a life on, isn't it?

God knew what He was doing from the beginning. He decided from the outset to shape the lives of those who love Him along the same lines as the life of His Son. Romans 8:29-30 says, "For those God foreknew He also predestined to be conformed to the likeness of His Son, that He might be the firstborn among many brothers. And those He predestined, He also called; those He called, He also justified; those He justified, He also glorified."

We look at this Son and see God's original purpose in everything created. "He is the image of the invisible God, the firstborn over all creation. For by Him all things were created: things in heaven and on earth, visible and invisible, whether thrones or powers or rulers or authorities, all things were created by Him and for Him" (Colossians 1:15-16).

Most of all let love guide your life. Colossians 3:14 says, "And over all these virtues put on love, which binds them all together in perfect unity. Let the peace of Christ rule in your hearts, since as members of one body you were called to peace."

YOU SHAPED ME

"For you created my innermost being; you knit me together in my mother's womb.

I praise you because I am fearfully and wonderfully made;

Your works are wonderful. I know that full well.

My frame was not hidden from you when I was made in the secret place.

When I was woven together in the depths of the earth,

Your eyes saw my unformed body.

All the days were ordained for me were written in your book

before one of them came to be."

(Psalm 139:13-16)

Self-Will

While I was deeply back into my very addictive days, I was able to actually stay clean and sober on my own for 18 months straight one time; and even another time I went for 4½ years without doing anything. No booze, no drugs, not even cigarettes! In all honesty here, I did have the hell of jail which forced me to get started on this sober road of 4½ years. However, my point in bringing this up here is that it did not last the test of time. Why? Here's the revelation I received from God on this: It has to do with where the power comes from. Even in AA/NA/CA 12-Step programs, and others you are taught that a power greater than oneself can restore us to sanity. A "power greater than oneself." I've also read a good number of self-help books, modules and materials and some are excellent and do help a lot of people in a lot of ways. So don't get me wrong here. Depending on what you're working on within yourself the self-help tools are wonderful. However, the true fix? The true fix comes from a higher power greater than ourselves. You see if self-help was all that was needed then we could just make a simple self-help decision and grab any and all of the tools we need to make those changes. Based on my experiences and from conversations I've had with others, self-help tools can work. Perhaps. But not for a lifetime, not permanently.

Consider this. I bought a totally hot conversion van. But the engine was no good. That's how I was able to afford it. It looked great and felt great to sit inside. But the engine was no good. So to move it anywhere I had to push it down the road a lot instead of using the bad engine. I was able to do this for a while and I was able to go short distances, but with each step I became more and more tired and drained of my power. I became frustrated, tired and then open for the devil to step in and attack me in my weakened state. I've learned our power is not enough for the long haul. Is there a better way? There has to be. The truth is there's only one way. One true source of pure power to truly change our lives for good and to maintain those positive changes. God through Jesus Christ!

We must surrender and be wholehearted in our love for Him, which gives us the power and perspectives we will need in our lives now and through eternity. Remember Jesus was once asked, "Teacher, which is the greatest commandment in the law?" And He said, "Love the Lord your God with all your heart and with all your soul and with all your mind." This is the first and greatest commandment, and the second is like it. "Love Your Neighbor as yourself." I believe Jesus knew what He was saying here. The more completely we love Him, the more complete our love for others will be, and that's the key. We've come full circle here. Without God's power found in a personal relationship with Him, found from Him by Him in love, remember Samson would have been just a tough guy hooked on weights and chicks; David just another dude with a wandering eye and no hope for forgiveness; Peter a mixed up fisherman who didn't know how to quit; Paul just a radical and John a forgotten old man with crazy dreams. But God's love and God's power was the true difference in these guys, right? So start making the right changes and trust God to supply the power as you need it. We know God also gives us the faith we need to face all of life's challenges and without faith we can't please Him, because common sense says anyone who comes to God must believe He exists and that He rewards those who earnestly seek Him. Therefore, if we seek God, trust Him to make all our necessary positive changes, He will faithfully do it for us and give us the power to make those changes reality. So as we now discover even more of God's love, a love so pure as pictured on the cross, our humility and gratitude comes automatically, doesn't it? As we grow more, and practice this love more with all our relationships, we will start to express in them what Jesus gave to all of us. True love.

We Keep It by Giving It Away
But You Can't Give What You Ain't Got!

"Love in deed is love indeed."

(John 3:16-18)

"Yet I hold this against you: You have forsaken your first love" (Revelation 2:4). Jesus, in Revelation, got into the church's face here. Not because they weren't doing a lot of good things, but because they (now get this) weren't doing the good things for the right reasons, "not out of love for Him!" Although they were praised for their patience, for their perseverance and for their deeds, from Jesus' view, they were being good for nothing. Resisting temptations, good deeds and behaviors, giving, forgiving, serving, teaching and loving should all be opportunities to express God's love and ours for Him. Remember, "We love Him because He first loved us" (John 4:19).

As soon as I made the decision to get out of my car that one day in the middle of the road and scream out "God Help Me" I began to slowly start understanding this love thing, and how God truly sees what's on and in our hearts and none of the external crap! By the way, I went to the hospital that day two minutes later, then to jail and then I got sober. So I tried in my own power to start giving back what I truly believed then and now - what God has given me. I made some real big goals and some real big plans how I will change the world. I even was voted the president of a recovery organization, opened a club, and did some good things for people and for kids of addicts. I even did some teaching in this area and facilitated inmates, serious inmates, in the areas of AODA (Alcohol and other Drug Addictions), along with Criminal Thinking Errors and Anger Management. Don't misunderstand me. I believe I did good for some people and maybe even today my stuff is still doing some good, but as I said I had big, big plans to walk in this kind of love so to speak. I wanted to, but it seemed I could not follow through. I made the elaborate plans but never carried them out or failed to. For one reason or another, mainly my addiction, I always got back into some trouble or another that would prevent me from following through with a goal or plan. So, of course then I would let the devil into my head. My unfulfilled goals or courses of action led to frustration and anger, even resentments. I would listen to my negative self-talk from Satan saying, "See, you aren't good enough. God doesn't want you." So then I would let this snowball into my self-esteem and my dissatisfaction with people, places and things and I would get harsh, judgmental, selfish, and on and on. And then it would all result in just using some more dope all over again. However, there is hope and here is the breakthrough, ok? The breakthrough is in His revelation within this book of God's love. None of us can truly and fully love one another until we accept and truly and fully receive His love for us. Oh, I believed it in my head, but these true changes have now just started to manifest in me when I put it into my heart. You see I was like a big vacuum. I had an urge to clean it up or help clean it up but I first had to clean my house and myself up better and I had to plug the damn vacuum into the true power source to perform what I needed and couldn't get on my own. Get it?

Christ's love creates unity in the midst of diversity.

Paul knew that God's love is a necessity. That we all have to have it or nothing will work out properly without this right formula, so to speak, no matter how noble we try to be, or how hard we try. Jesus taught the churches about giving for all the wrong reasons and Paul prayed for the church to know God and deep true love by living it.

"That Christ may dwell in your hearts by faith, that ye, being rooted and grounded in love may be able to comprehend with all saints what is the breadth, and length, and depth and height and to know the love of Christ which passeth knowledge that ye might be filled with all the fullness of God" (Ephesians 3:17-20).

WOW.

So we see right relationships are based solely on love. Now once we begin to receive God's unconditional love for us, not only can we begin to start loving Him back in return, but we can also now begin to truly start fully loving others. Now we can give it back. Now we truly have something to give.

"Herein is love, not that we loved God, but that He loved us and sent His son to be the propitiation (the sacrifice) for our sins" (1 John 4:10).

"Beloved, if God so loved us, we ought also to love one another" (1 John 4:11).

Now as we have the love of God in us we can give it away. We can choose to love others unconditionally as God taught us and is teaching us today, and every day in this same way, as He has loved us. We all want to be accepted, needed, wanted, desired and to be loved. This love, this wonderful gift from God to us – how it truly just flows to us and then through us – to all others. Now can you start to see how this book will change your life?" I knew that you would!

This love is an effort but don't forget, and I pray that we don't get lazy in giving it out to all. Stay on course and keep giving back the main meaning in our lives. Love. Love. Love.

SHEAVES OF GRAIN

Love makes obedience a thing of joy!
To do the will of one we like to please
Is never hardship, though it tax our strength
Each privilege of service love will seize,
Love makes us loyal, glad to do our goal,
And eager to defend a name or cause,
Love takes the drudgery from common work
and asks no rich reward or great applause.
Love gives us satisfaction in our task and wealth
in learning lessons of the heart.
Love sheds a light of glory on our toll and makes
us humbly glad to have a part.

Author: Hazel Hartwell Simon

Book 6

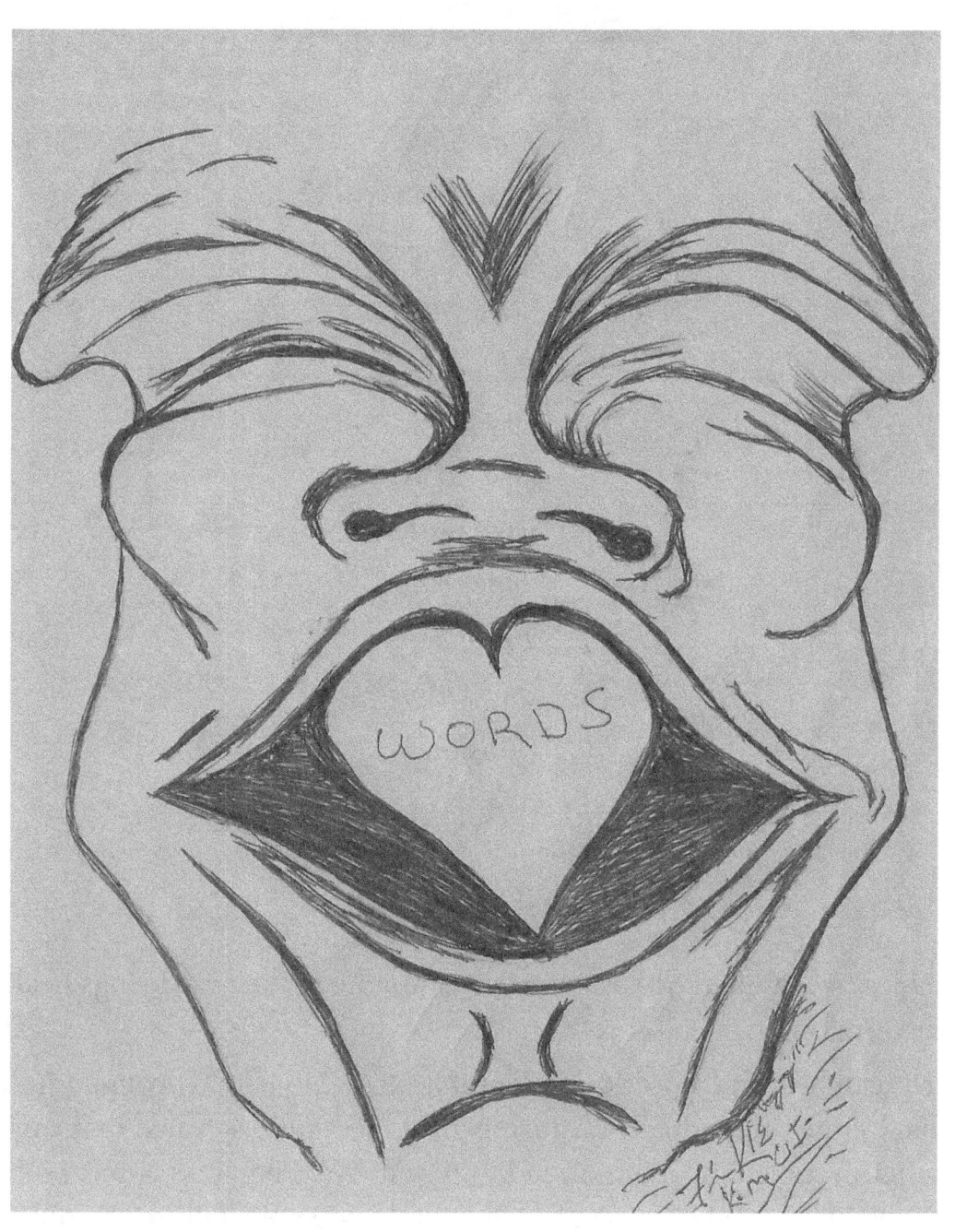

Watch Your Mouth

One look.

One smile.

One touch.

One embrace.

One kiss.

One love.

Two people.

Two minds.

Two destinies.

One road.

One journey.

One ending.

Together.

Author: Melissa Higgins

"Reckless words pierce like a sword, but tongue of the wise brings healing" (Proverbs 12:18).

Words can heal and words can kill and destroy. No joke. Throughout the world, people have either individually or during group sessions, revealed that words of harsh criticism spoken by mom or dad were remembered years later, and their lives were badly affected because of it. Being told you are a failure by your parents stays with you. Many groups, including groups involving prisoners, share their own stories that have left them with deep internal wounds. Serious wounds that can cut deeply. It takes a long time to heal. Some never do. Some do heal, but only by the grace of God's unconditional love. So we really have to watch our mouths. We can and should use our mouths for blessing, healing and building up others, not cursing or bullying others. Being positive attracts positives by the way. Parents should not tell their kids that they are this or that unless it is what they want them to be. Why? Because words create a long lasting impact or image within us. "For as he thinketh in his heart so is he. Eat and drink saith he to thee but his heart is not with thee" (Proverbs 23:7).

"Do not be deceived: God cannot be mocked. A man reaps what he sows" (Galatians 6:7).

I'll share a little story or two here to try and make a point. When I was a child I went to Catholic schools for 7th, 8th and 9th grade. We moved around a lot so this was already the fourth or fifth school I went to for 7th grade. Being the new kid is never easy. Needless to say, I was a bit of a class clown and the kid that would always take a dare, you know to try to fit in with the other kids. Acceptance. Trying to fill the void. We talked about this in earlier chapters. Well, anyway, I was the first kid to wear bell bottom jeans to school. Not only were they bell bottom jeans, they were the red, white and blue flag-colored bell bottom jeans in 7th grade at a Catholic school that wore uniforms. I believe I was also the first kid to be punched in the mouth by a priest for being a smartass. So I know a little about what words can do and their effects. Also, I remember around the same time I called my mom a bitch. I had learned this new word and didn't really know what it meant, but thought I was cool and a big shot so I said it to my mom in front of some other kids as I was trying to show off. Well, my father, who popped in for one of his rare weekend visits, found out about this and took me downstairs for one of our "beating me" sessions because I used this word. I mention this to raise an important point. One is that it's just a word. Look at the word and how it is being used today. You see it on t-shirts and other clothing and you hear it on the radio and television all the time. The word is often used in comedy skits. The word was wrong then and it is wrong to be used now.

Sticks and stones do break our bones, but words can wound more deeply.

The Bible and God's teachings are the same today as they were 2000 years ago. And by the way, I have to mention here that the "b" word never described my mother. She was the most loving person in the world and a wonderful mother. A saint as far as I'm concerned.

How we talk, how we act, how we dress, all of it, falls under time honored standards. Many years ago, I watched one of those late night shows, I think it was David Letterman. The guest he had on was a very rich and popular pop star who sang pretty well and seemed intelligent enough. She told Letterman that all she had to do was wear very little clothing wherever she went. She also professed her faith in Jesus. Friends, the principles in the Bible are not "old school." They are timeless.

The Bible says that words cut like a two-edged sword.

"In like manner also, that women adorn themselves in modest apparel, with shamefacedness and sobriety, not with braided hair, or gold, or pearls or costly array" (1 Timothy 2:9). We should not talk or dress to draw attention to ourselves. Like I did in school, and like the use of certain words is clearly doing today.

"And be not conformed to this world, but be ye transformed by the renewing of your mind, that ye may prove what is that good, and acceptable and perfect will of God" (Romans 12:2). So let's choose our words and actions carefully. Remember words, like actions, are seeds that will grow one way or another. It's easy to find something wrong in people and in things. But love (our new love) covers all of it. All the faults it covers are the sins as well.

"Above all, love each other deeply because love covers over a multitude of sins" (1 Peter 4:8).

If we want to start to make this love a habit, then we must also develop the new habit of loving people with our words. Again, as we said the world loves to point out our flaws as they see them. It's human nature to make ourselves feel better by tearing down others. But what we're actually doing is magnifying our own faults instead of doing what we are supposed to do and that is cover these faults, big or small, with our love. Romans 12:21 says, "Be not overcome of evil, but overcome evil with good."

It is easy to find something wrong with everyone, but love covers it. As stated in 1 Peter 4:8-11, "Above all, love each other deeply, because love covers over a multitude of sins. Offer hospitality to one another without grumbling. Each one should use whatever gift he has received to serve others, faithfully administering God's grace in its various forms. If anyone speaks, he should do it as one speaking the very words of God. If anyone serves, he should do it with the strength God provides so that in all things God may be praised through Jesus Christ to Him be the glory and the power for ever and ever. Amen."

"But I tell you that men will have to give account on the Day of Judgment for every careless word they have spoken."

(Matthew 12:36)

Just Things

"On such love, my soul still ponder. Love so great, so rich, so free. Say, while lost in holy wonder, why Oh Lord, such love to me?"

Verse 4 of Hymn Sovereign Grace O'er Sin Abounding

Lyrics by John Kent

Saying something is one thing. Thinking something is another thing. But doing something, well now, that's a whole other bag of worms here, isn't it?

"Dear children, let us not love with words or tongue but with actions and in truth. This then is how we know that we belong to the truth, and how we set our hearts at rest in His presence whenever our hearts condemn us. For God is greater than our hearts, and He knows everything" (1 John 3:18-20).

We all love cars, boats, planes, trains, trucks, clothes, jewelry, shoes, toys, and other things. The list is endless, right? There are times in our lives (if we are telling the truth) that we might do something risky or dangerous just to get something we really wanted. Maybe we even lied, cheated, stole, or used someone to get what we wanted. I know I have. I love things and I used people to get them. However, it's important to know that God on the other hand wants us to love people and use things to bless them. So by giving of our things or sharing our things with people we actually go from talking or thinking about doing a good deed (showing love) to actually doing the good deed.

When I was in a program it took me a very long time to admit I was powerless over drugs, and get this, that's not even the true reality of it. I was so hard-headed, arrogant and full of pride, I couldn't admit I was powerless over anything. Yet this is the very first thing you must do here, ok? Now here's the catch. Not only do you have to admit it, it's not until you actually accept it that you can begin to do something about it, right? I can admit until I'm blue in the face that I'm powerless.

But until I take the action of accepting it where it then goes from my head, from my thinking or just words to my heart where I truly believe it, then and only then can I do something about it. God has given us a heart of compassion. But by our own bad choices, we prevent it from working smoothly at times. We choose to open or close the flow. We must stop hindering God from doing what He wants and that is to work His great love through each of us. There are no other expressions of our lives and of our faith more important. "For God gave us a spirit not of fear but of power and love and self-control" (2 Timothy 1:17).

Our God wants to express His great heart of love through us. So you see all this other great stuff that we're talking about doing, achieving in our growth and in our lives, none of it will amount to anything without the true meaning of our lives, and what is that true meaning of life? You're getting it, that's right, to love, love, love.

To love our neighbor as ourselves is not an easy thing to do.
So Lord, please show us how to love, as we attempt to follow You.

"Do not love the world or anything in the world. If anyone love the world, the love of the Father is not in Him" (1 John 2:15).

"For to their power I bear record, yea, and beyond their power they were willing of themselves" (2 Corinthians 8:3).

The Act of Love

"Actions speak louder than words."

Abraham Lincoln

Let's remember to love each other, not things. God gave us everything in the first place and He did it for us to share anyway. We know, however, through life's experiences that people have taken their greed for material things as far as it can go. People have killed and are killing today for things. Things we don't even take with us when we go, right? So this is no joke here and a serious point.

Live to Give

We also must learn to push this issue and stretch ourselves because it's not always easy to give. We must learn to get out of our comfort zones on a lot of the issues I've talked about. Giving away something we can spare or can afford to give away is one thing; giving something that you can't is another. Why do we know we should take it to this new painful level? Like, for instance, giving away your only means of transportation, your new car. Now this will hurt some, right? Why don't we know it's the right thing to do? Didn't Jesus Christ give in a far greater way when He gave His life for our sins?

"For we brought nothing into the world and it is certain we can carry nothing out" (1 Timothy 6:7).

"No pain no gain."

Ben Franklin

"For the love of money is a root of all kinds of evil. Some people, eager for money, have wandered from the faith and pierced themselves with many griefs" (1 Timothy 6:10).

Please don't get me wrong. God does in fact want us to be plentiful and enjoy all the world has to offer. He delights in it as a matter of fact. "Give and it will be given to you. A good measure, pressed down, shaken together and running over, will be poured into your lap. For with the measure you use, it will be measured to you" (Luke 6:38).

God did not bring us this far to let us go now. He's not done yet so pay attention. We are all called together by God to first be blessed and then be a blessing to others. "I will make you into a great nation, and I will bless you. I will make your name great and you will be a blessing" (Genesis 12:2).

To repeat, in all things we first must take it from our heads to our hearts. Then our motives are pure and of God. If our motive is to be a blessing, it proves God's point and proves you can be trusted with money and possessions. Also, a good rule of thumb is we reap what we sow. "As long as the earth endures, seedtime and harvest, cold and heat, summer and winter, day and night will never cease" (Genesis 8:22). While the earth God created still exists don't ever forget that God knows what's truly on the heart and we should avoid giving with the only motive of getting something back. Our Number One motive for giving should be as a blessing to someone. Primarily we should help those less fortunate than us. We should bless the needy and the poor, but not lose sight of the fact that we're all equal under God's eyes and the rich need our blessings also. Sometimes even more. Regardless of how much you give the act of giving is the most important part. There are other ways to give besides gifts we can see or touch. Words of encouragement is an example of an emotional gift. This is just as important as material gifts.

What it comes down to is this. It isn't the amount that truly matters or makes the blessing and difference in someone's life. It is in the act of love that is needed. I'll say it again. It is the act of love that makes the true difference in the lives of people we're giving to. The blessing is in the internal knowledge they feel from the inside on the heart. The act of love to heal, help and bless them. The act of love that can and will make the difference in their lives and in our world as a whole.

This to the End, that our great
Blessings may never spoil us,
That we shall forever live in
Thankful contemplation
Of Him who presides
Over us
All…

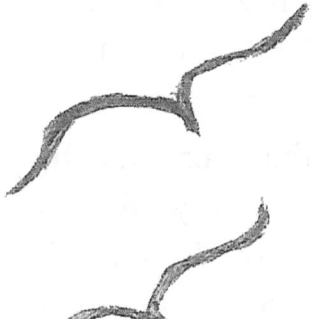

Book 7

Love

French is considered to be a very romantic language, but there are many words in the English language that are very nice and smooth. Some seem to just roll off the tongue like the word "lullaby" or how about "lucidity." Out of all the words that exist, the word "love" is the most emotional, powerful and sweetest word. We never really understand it. We can't see it, or touch it or grab hold of it. We don't seem to truly admit it or even know how to accept it and we're all afraid. Yes, we're all afraid to express it mainly for fear of being hurt by it. Still we all want it, need it or long for the chance, yes, and just one chance to truly experience it.

Because of the mighty need, want or quest for this crazy little thing called love, I believe it's most important to understand some of the very things we do that prevents and keeps us from this important element. Love is that which we seek and fear simultaneously. I've studied many books on the subject of love. Psychologists, psychiatrists, doctors, teachers, theologians, and others all have various theories, some more complex than others, of why some people have difficulty allowing themselves to love, feel or accept love from others. Why some people with backgrounds of deep personal trauma or negative emotional feelings seem so reluctant to break through or step past the walls that would allow them to feel love or express love to other people. My own experience was that I had to literally beat myself into surrender, to just get myself to the basic first steps in this important process of life. There are many approaches, some medical, some psychological, to help people who suffer from this. One thing I know for sure is that a conscious definite decision for a person to make a change in beliefs or values in learned behaviors has to occur. The person who has suffered deep wounds, perhaps from a childhood experience, is the only person who can break through the walls. Perhaps by giving themselves permission to feel and to allow love into their lives. Too often we set up our own roadblocks which stops or hinders our hope of experiencing love, a feeling that is the reason for life itself. As we gain a clearer perspective of our lives, we can also gain a true perspective of our lives as God ordained it. We can see that God's love for us is true love, not of our own understanding. Here are my own feelings, my own favorite expressions of love:

- Even though I believe love at first sight exists and is powerful, I believe it is even more remarkable when people, who have put up with all the faults of each other for many years, have a love that continues to grow for each other.

- There is a void, a hole or emptiness in the heart of everyone that can't be filled with any created thing, but only by the creator – God.

- Look here my friends, death is and was never the intended end, but a part and time, a mere event in our lives and for some a fresh new beginning for even more wisdom of an even purer love.

- I fully guarantee that if and when you do an inventory of your life, you will find that the times you truly lived and that truly mattered are times when you acted in the spirit of love.

Now here are some other beautiful expressions of love by people over the centuries:

"Love seeketh not to please nor for itself has any care, but for another gives its ease, and builds a heaven in hell's despair."

William Blake

"He that shuts love out, in turn shall be shut out from love and on her threshold lie, howling in outer darkness."

Alfred Lord Tennyson

"To love is to admire with the heart – to admire is to love with the mind."

Theophile Gautier

"A loving heart is the truest wisdom."

Charles Dickens

"Love is a fruit in season at all times, and within the reach of every hand."

Mother Teresa

"Love is the master key which opens the gates of happiness."

Oliver Wendell Holmes

"Love is most nearly itself when here and now cease to matter."

T.S. Eliot

"Love gives itself, it is not bought."

Henry Wadsworth Longfellow

"Love is the only force capable of transforming an enemy into a friend."

Martin Luther King

"Love feels no burden, thinks nothing of trouble, attempts what is above its strength, pleads no excuse of impossibility, for it thinks all things lawful for itself and all things possible."

Thomas A. Kempis

"Love is a better teacher than duty."

Albert Einstein

"Love is space and time measured by the heart."

Marcel Proust

"Love is the only weapon we need."

Rev. H.R.L. Sheppard

"Take away love and our earth is a tomb."

Robert Browning

"Love is energy of life."

Robert Browning

> *"To love at all is to be vulnerable. Love anything and your heart will certainly be wrung and possibly be broken. If you want to make sure of keeping it intact, you must give your heart to no one, not even to an animal. Wrap it carefully around with hobbies and little luxuries; avoid all entanglements; lock it up safe in the casket or coffin of your selfishness. But in that casket – safe, dark, motionless, airless – it will change. It will not be broken; it will become unbreakable, impenetrable, and irredeemable."*
>
> *C.S. Lewis*

Below are some passages from the Bible about love that Jesus spoke:

"A new command I give you: Love one another. As I have loved you, so you must love one another" (John 13:34).

"But I tell you who hear me: Love your enemies, do good to those who hate you. Bless those who curse you, pray for those who mistreat you" (Luke 6:27-28).

"If you love me, you will obey what I command" (John 14:15).

"So in everything, do to others what you would have them do to you, for this sums up the Law and the Prophets" (Matthew 7:12).

"And when you stand praying, if you hold anything against anyone, forgive him, so that your Father in heaven may forgive you your sins" (Mark 11:25).

"Let no debt remain outstanding, except the continuing debt to love one another, for he who loves his fellowman has fulfilled the law" (Romans 13:8).

God makes it very clear, doesn't He? To continue the point, here are ten additional scripture references about love:

"Earnestly pursue love and eagerly desire spiritual gifts, especially the gift of prophecy" (1 Corinthians 14:1).

"Whereas the object and purpose of our instruction and charge is love which springs from a pure heart and a good conscience and sincere faith" (1 Timothy 1:5).

"Pursue faith, love and peace together with those who worship the Lord with a pure heart" (2 Timothy 2:22).

"Let brotherly love continue" (Hebrews 13:1).

"Above all, love each other deeply, because love covers over a multitude of sins" (1 Peter 4:8).

"Beloved, let us love one another for love is of God and every one that loveth is born of God, and knoweth God" (1 John 4:7).

"And the Lord directs your heart into the love of God and into the patient waiting for Christ" (2 Thessalonians 3:5).

"The Lord thy God in the midst of thee is mighty; He will save, He will rejoice over thee with joy; He will rest in His love; He will joy over thee with singing" (Zephaniah 3:17).

"And over all these virtues put on love, which binds them all together in perfect unity" (Colossians 3:14).

"Whoever has my commandments and obeys them, he is the one who loves me. He who loves me will be loved by my Father and I too will love him and show myself to him" (John 14:21).

BEATITUDES OF LOVE

Blessed are they who find love everywhere, for they may never be lonely.

Blessed are they who make it easier for others to love them,

For they shall always have plenty of friends.

Blessed are those who are always communicating love,

For they are channels of blessing wherever they go.

Blessed are those who bestow healing love,

For they may be known as the physicians of the soul.

Blessed are those who leave love wherever they go,

For the world will be a better place because they have lived.

Blessed are those who love to work for theirs is the kingdom of service.

Blessed are those who love to share, for theirs is the kingdom of joy everywhere.

Blessed are those who love to wait, for theirs is the kingdom of patience.

Blessed are those who love to praise others, for theirs is the kingdom of appreciation.

Blessed are those who love to put others first, for theirs is the kingdom of humility.

Blessed are those who love to be courteous, for theirs is the kingdom of good manners.

Blessed are those who love God first, and above all,

For theirs is the kingdom of right relationship to God, people and things.

Blessed are those who love Jesus Christ,

For they share His tender compassion for the whole world.

Blessed are those who love and receive the Holy Spirit, for theirs is the Kingdom of holiness.

Blessed are those who practice love in relation to people at all times,

For theirs is the kingdom of intimate kindness.

Blessed are those who plan to practice love always, for they shall live in the house of love and dwell in the city of God forever and ever.

Author: Thomas A. Charruth

Fresh Start

This new beginning, this fresh start, this new birth is only the beginning of an ultimately different life and world for us all. With this new ultimate loving relationship with our God, just keep your eyes on the prize as we grow in it. How totally exciting. Yet it will and does take a commitment. However, with His help and strength, we endure life on life's terms and pressures, and overcome and step through our self-inflicted walls. We will now start to feel, see and experience the tremendous wonders God has in store. Now get this, whether we do it willingly or not, or struggle and fight our whole life against this, the fact is the things of this world will in fact no doubt just fade away. To experience the whole fullness of God's joy for us now and through eternity we must realize this; that we not only have to surrender completely; we not only have to let it all go and let God, we must also start shifting all our focus. Yes. All our focus, off all the temporary "stuff" of this world to the wonderful "stuff" of an eternal world. To God Himself. To the essence of love.

"The Lord's love never ends. His mercies never stop. They are new every morning."

(Lamentations 3:22-23)

God's Love in Everything from The Beginning
The Basic True Facts
God is the Beginning, the End and So Much in Between!

God is faithful, eternal, all knowing, just, unchangeable, gracious, holy, merciful, long-suffering, impartial and infinite.

God is Perfect

God is all powerful, almighty, personal, righteous, unsearchable, wise, triune, accessible, self-existent, glorious and compassionate.

God is Perfect

God is Creator, He is Redeemer, He is shepherd, He is savior, Lord and Father, He is Judge, He is comforter, He is teacher, He is I Am, He is the mighty one.

God is Perfect

God is our shield, our stronghold, our light, our sustainer, our rescuer, our fortress. He is Love.

God is Perfect

Why would we choose anything else? Why? I Choose Love.

God's love is shown in all things, always. All the time.

Almost everything we see on a daily basis makes it so very clear we have a perfect God and a loving God. The more we try to prove otherwise the more we learn that all things are for a purpose in everything God has created from the beginning. Here are a few examples of what I'm trying to tell you. In Milwaukee, abandoned and unused office buildings are being turned into condominiums. In Colorado, the oldest wooden aircraft hangar built in 1919 remains in its original location, but it is now an 8700 square foot, open air versatile event space. In Philadelphia, funds continue to be raised by a preservation group to raise money to renovate a rusty old battleship and turn it into a waterfront complex. Each structure at one time had a specific use, but one that is no longer relevant. Still, someone was able to see a new purpose for each one.

Now, let's look at a little different kind of God's touches.

Enter and view God's works and God's touches. Consider the rainforests of Brazil, the beauty of the Reindeer Glacier in Greenland, the majesty of the Grand Canyon in Arizona, or perhaps just the flow of wheat fields as the wind blows over them. Think of Niagara Falls or the New York Botanical Gardens, the Atlantic or Pacific Ocean, the Isle of Capri in Italy; the list is endless and the expression of God's love so apparent. How awesome and beautiful are these gifts He has given us? Consider the many kinds of flowers there are – roses, lilies, tulips, endless varieties. Consider the many kinds of trees. In North America alone, there are over 1000 different types of trees native to America. This is according to Thomas Pakenham who wrote a book called Remarkable Trees of the World. Have you ever seen the Redwood Forest in California? The Redwood trees are the tallest trees on the planet, reaching as tall as 350 feet, and they can live for 2000 years. What unbelievable love and breathtaking beauty that God has given us.

Here's a quick little story about a girl I knew back in my drug-using days. She had a guy she messed around with to get money for dope. This guy's family owned a big suburban jewelry store chain and she was a jewelry maker. Well, one day I saw her and she ran up to me and put a beautiful ring, shaped as a woman's body, on my finger and said she made it for me. I found out later that she took all the scraps that the guy's father would throw away after sizing rings and she made me a thing of beauty. Isn't it amazing what a master craftsman can do with what we might view as no good, of no value or useless?

Just know that we're all fixable. We are all put here for a valuable purpose, a perfect plan of a perfect God whose love is so apparent in all things. We are all a true product of a master craftsman. He takes all the many wasted pieces and broken links of our lives and will always recycle them and restore them to their worth and pure meaning, no matter how far we backslide. I've slid backwards way too many times in so many different ways, yet God's love has seen fit to wait me out and be patient with me and continue to show me a better way. His way of Love. And He is doing that for you as well. If structures can find new productive life, then so can people. Don't you think God took a little more time for people? Remember in an earlier chapter when we discussed the many men of the Bible whose lives took an unexpected direction? Remember Jacob, who fought with the angel of the Lord, and Moses who talked to a burning bush. Paul who was temporarily blinded – all their stories and our stories were different. But were they?

Isn't the end result starting to look a little familiar to you? Yes, these stories were all a little different but what was surely true is this. All of these people eventually had a change. A change of meaning, of purpose when their encounters with God sent them down a new road to travel or a new path. No matter what mistakes we make, and believe me, I've made plenty, God can and will remold us into clean vessels that are all good in His eyes.

It's all good as we confess our sins and submit ourselves to step toward more and more obedience to His Word. We allow God's love to do what He wanted to do all along, to fix us to do His redemptive work in our lives. We are reminded that love is the only way for the pieces of all our broken lives to be made good and full and whole. God reminds us of this in John 15:9 which says, "As the Father has loved me, so have I loved you. Now remain in my love." And again in Jeremiah 29:11-13 which says, "For I know the plans I have for you, plans to prosper you and not to harm you, plans to give you hope and a future. Then you will call upon me and come and pray to me, and I will listen to you. You will seek me and find me when you seek me with all your heart."

"Cast all your anxiety on Him because He cares for you. Be self-controlled and alert. Your enemy, the devil prowls around like a roaring lion looking for someone to devour. Resist him, standing firm in the faith, because you know that your brothers throughout the world are undergoing the same kind of sufferings. And the God of all grace who called you to His eternal glory in Christ, after you have suffered a little while, will Himself restore you and make you strong, firm and steadfast. To Him be the power for ever and ever. Amen" (1 Peter 5:7-11).

Book 8

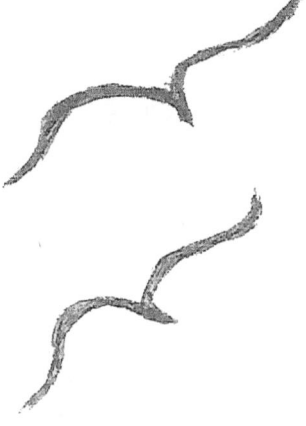

Child of a deathless morn
You were not ever born.
You will not ever die
For time is mind's ancient lie.
Its fleeting fancy's pass
Across minds looking glass
Forever old and new
No child of time are you.
But through eternity
You are and will be.
And have the meaning whole
Already in your soul.

Author: Frank (1979)

The Most Insane of People Can Be Used to Help Us All Get to That Better Place

"Time, time, time is on my side. Yes it is."

Excerpt from song <u>Time is on My Side</u>

written by Norman Meade and performed by The Rolling Stones.

My name is Frank and I'm a recovering person. At the risk of showing my old age, it was 1974, my last year of high school; back then we beat up cars that today sell for $100,000. Gas averaged 53 cents per gallon. Gerald Ford was president. John Lennon was already under the influence of Yoko Ono, among other things, and the Beatles had broken up. Elvis was alive and making my mom cry with songs like Love Me Tender. Mark David Chapman comes up for parole in 2022 for the murder of John Lennon in 1980. He has previously been denied parole eleven times. All this seems like a long time ago. Like a brief look over my shoulder.

There are, however, other ways to perceive time. As you sit in an 8' high cell 23 hours a day, time will take on a far different meaning, right? I guess my point here is perception. The perception of what time can do. For example, what it may do to give you that corroding of the human heart. Or the time passed and the never ending shadows it throws upon today, in the present; shadows where others hold it all against you forever and even cast bigger exaggerated darkness upon you to make the story better or to make their life seem better. This sort of thing keeps getting worse and grows and grows. Which now brings me to a strong point as I share some heavy things about myself briefly and for the reason of this book.

Beginning with Book One of this book, I hope we have gotten a far better understanding of the Number One question, which is, "what's the meaning of life?" I believe we decided that love is the answer, or should be. Right? Well, in the chapters that follow I hope to answer some heavy questions as well that everyone wonders about. If there is a God, how and why would He allow tragedies to happen? For example a small child being molested and killed. Would a true loving God allow this? So stay with me and keep reading. Some of my many experiences are as follows and is why I'm compelled to write the following:

Who knows the feelings of physical and/or emotional abuse? I do.

Who knows or truly understands the loss of a child? I do.

Who knows the heartache of having a home split apart at a very young age? I do.

Who knows the pain of someone you love kill themselves in front of you? I do.

Who knows the feeling of your best friend for fifty years come down with Alzheimer's and forget who you are? I do.

Who knows the miseries of being a teen addicted to drugs? I do.

Who knows the pain of being misunderstood and being sent to prison for it? I do.

Now I could continue with more examples but I've said in earlier chapters, I want to get to the meaning of all this and to the solutions and not dwell on the problems. Let's just say experience is the best teacher and pain is a hell of a motivation. I've had my fill of both.

Time and Chaos

We live in a world of friction and pain, conflict and a lot of suffering. But I do not want you to think I'm putting down the world. I'm not. It is a great big wonderful world in which we live. A world that was truly a magnificent gift from God. I sincerely believe we can get rid of the negative issues if we work together. Then we can enjoy the gift of peace and love together.

The passage of time and the continued chaos in the world has not changed my hopes, plans or concerns. At least not completely. My underlying beliefs and moral values have only gained strength. I still believe God knows what is on our hearts and I still believe in the human heart and its unbelievable strength and power. And without a doubt, as we learned in the first part of this book, I believe in the essential validity of love as the most powerful and pure emotion. And it is the only emotion we carry over with us from here to eternity. What else can we take from this world to the next?

I also still have faith that connections can and are made between people, and that occasionally our spirits on earth will touch so we can continue to understand they are still okay, and so much more is still in front of us to experience. I also believe that the price of this knowledge can be very costly. I believe the true value of this cost outweighs the price. The price must, and through and because of God will be paid. I still believe in good vs. evil and we all must find our place to stand and then defend that place to the end.

At every step our kids should be able and be allowed to deal with real experiences of our lives, and the thorns must not ever be plucked from their roses.

Why All the F**king Pain?

Are you ready for some truth? Here we go again. If you are just barely getting by, barely able to deal with the small pressures of life when things are peaceful, going along with the everyday nuts of the grounds, what then are you going to do when the little problems start hitting the fan, let alone the bigger, harder stuff? What about when the real warfare starts up? God wants us all to be properly prepared for what He has planned for us. He wants us prepared for the days of afflictions. He wants all of us not only prepared but protected.

"If you have run with footmen and they have tired you out, then how can you compete with horses? If you fall down in a land of peace, how will you do in the thickets of the Jordan?" (Jeremiah 12:5)

As for me for far too long, I compromised a lot of my own thoughts, my values and even my beliefs to try to fit into man's world of the flesh. So I say to all of you now, what are we measuring ourselves against? Think of it all like the learning curve from our days in school. If everyone did badly the percentage or grade point average you needed to pass was decreased. So if the morals and standards of society go down, we go down with it. Or do we try to do something to bring up our brothers and sisters?

I once went to jail and while I was in what they call the bullpen area waiting to see the Judge, I could not help but compare myself and the reason I was there. I would tell myself that I wasn't violent and my crime wasn't as bad as someone else's crime. Yet what I was doing was measuring myself against a room full of criminals. What would the result have been if I measured myself and my crime against a room full of responsible people? Get my point? The world is changing and the church is compromising more and more. We are compromising more and more. We must get back on track before it is too late.

Now here's a valid point to understand because if we believe in the Bible and that God is in total control from the beginning to the end, like I do, then we must believe that God causes or brings about what is specifically appointed for each and every one of us. This suffering that I faced, in fact all suffering that we face must be and is exactly as God designed it. Now please understand this. We will never learn the true lessons God wants us to until we get this point. Don't get me wrong here as we continue this line of thought. I don't even come close to pretending I have all the answers or know even a small portion of God's ultimate wisdom or knowledge. But I have been blessed throughout the good and bad experiences in my life. Good and bad passed on some understandings from God or from other people. Like I said in the first part of this book, if we treat our lives like a relay race and we pass the baton forward from where we left off instead of making our kids start over or get their wisdom and understandings on their own, we would be a lot further and closer to where God wants us to be by now.

Now back to the question of suffering and pain. Like I said, I'm sure God has plenty more reasons to allow our pain and our sufferings, but I'll talk about a few reasons I do understand clearly. I will not talk or attempt to teach about something I'm not sure of. That would just get us nowhere.

"God whispers in our pleasures but shouts in our pain."

Author: C.S. Lewis

From his book, The Problem of Pain

The Bible teaches us that God and God Himself admits He is the God of all comfort.

So then it's safe to say God allows us to suffer so we can learn to comfort others as He has comforted us. He comforts regardless of any circumstances big or small, bad or good. Pain is His concern and specialty. Paul said it like this in 2 Corinthians 1:11, "Blessed be God the Father of our Lord Jesus Christ, the Father of mercies and God of all comfort; who comforts us in all our affliction so that we may be able to comfort those who are in any affliction with the comfort with which we ourselves are comforted by God."

A friend or loved one dying of cancer. The heartache of a broken home. A teen on dope living with a junkie. Failure in school or at work. Who on this earth truly understands these issues? Answer: The people going through it! So this is one of the reasons why we suffer. To be able to bring hope, faith, love, encouragement and comfort to those we meet who are going through the same thing. Let's look a little deeper and see the ripple effect. We go through the pain. God always comes along and comforts us. Someone else suffers, we step up and comfort them. God's hand in ours. Our hand in others. Understand?

Let's discuss another powerful reason we suffer and go through pain. In earlier chapters of this book, I spoke about literally having to beat myself into a position of surrender before I could finally start getting to the truth. I'll get into a lot more of this later on but I will say when I first got into an AODA program many years ago, they had some steps one must follow. So, being the hardheaded intellectual human being that I am, I had to prove my points or prove them wrong. The very first words in the steps of this program were, "We admitted we were powerless." So of course I would dissect this into a million pieces to justify how it did not apply to me. To admit, that's just words. To accept, now that's something else. Can you see how this can keep us stuck in the same place a long time?

Thus, finally surrendering to something or someone else's way of doing things is important and of course, this took a whole lot of pain. So the next powerful point here is that we must suffer and go through pain in order to learn to not trust in ourselves alone. So as I have done, we must beat ourselves into submission to completely realize that we are nothing without God. We need God in all things. You see when we hit bottom or come to a complete emptying of "self" we can learn the power of total dependence on God. As I said in earlier chapters, "pain = motivation." Taking it a step further we see that pain gets us to fully understand that we all need others and are in need of help from something outside of ourselves. John 15:5 says, "I am the vine, you are the branches. He who abides in me, and I in him, bears much fruit; for without me you can do nothing."

Just as I have asked myself many, many times, I ask you now. How much longer are we going to fight God? I know from my experience that He's not going to give up on me. He wants total dependence. Our total submission to Him so He can bless us with His infinite wisdom and His unconditional love. The bottom line is the pain shows our true self status. We're not all powerful or all smart. But guess what? God is. We're in need of Him. We need to take everything we were and we ever hoped to be and just give it all to God.

> *"Be still and know that I am God: I will be exalted among the nation; I will be exalted in the earth."*
>
> *(Psalm 46:10)*

Now a little more on the very important question as to why God allows tragedy, suffering and pain. If we truly believe that God is the conductor of all our experiences both good and bad, joy and suffering, and that we go through it so we can better be prepared to comfort others, then we should begin to have a deeper appreciation for this awesome loving God and start to truly begin to give thanks in everything. Because of many people, including Paul, in the Bible and the afflictions and pain, we were always led to believe we should focus on the Lord Jesus Christ. When we offer praise in our moments of sorrow God has to smile for He knows now we're starting to get it. Even God used this type of revelation and learning process with Jesus himself. Didn't He suffer as well? As a matter of fact at one point did He not suffer for the sins of all mankind? All mankind all at once. Can you imagine the pain and suffering He endured? Let's all begin to thank Him more for us even being considered a part, big or small, of His almighty plan.

Thank you God for the pain. For we now are beginning to get a clearer and fuller understanding of Your plan and Your love for us. We have learned hate to better appreciate love. We have learned sadness to better appreciate joy. We have learned anxiety to better appreciate peace. We now have no doubt of this as well, that out of all suffering comes good because this suffering is used by You. We know nothing enters our life by accident or by luck or any other way unless You allow it. We're learning that behind every living experience God is there to continue to mold and shape us, and that when God wants to do an incredible impossibly thinking task to meet His plan, He will use an impossible person like me or you to do it. The Bibles proves this. Just look at the type of people God used. Moses, Paul, Peter, John. All had some not so credible or righteous lives until God finally got their attention. There are thousands just like them. Like me. Like you.

*It isn't the tranquil and calm seas that brings out the true sailor's skills.
It's the wind and waves that pound his ship and toss it about at will.*

Getting Little, Getting Low

In earlier chapters of this book, we discover and come to realize that love is the most essential and powerful purpose for our lives. This unconditional love that comes from God is powerful enough to cover absolutely anything we come across on the face of this Earth and beyond. We are getting closer now to truly beginning to see the mighty results of God's love. Let me say this one more time so it sinks in. We are truly about to start seeing the mighty powerful results of God's love. You remember the old saying, "you ain't seen nothing yet."

LIKE A CHILD

My children, I know you don't get it all. It's too big for your mind.

But believe your Father, your God desires and works with an infinite love and an infinite power.

We are all about to see this love in action, not just as in the past with all the miracles or revivals and the touching and sovereign powers that hit all people, families, churches, cities, states and nations. Yes, we have seen some powerful stuff but again "we ain't seen nothing yet." God's going to restore this earth, His world, our world to rid it of all darkness. In Him is love enough to cast out all hatred from the entire world and to bring us all to a new peace and love. And He would love to have our assistance. The question is simple. Are we in or out?

Know this, that all our children learn through our learned beliefs so they will always be more likely to live up to what we believe in them.

Here are some things we must do now to allow our God to better prepare us for this work. First we see a clearer understanding of our past stupidities. In earlier chapters of this book I said when you know better and yet you keep making the same mistakes over and over, are you not more insane than the people that don't know yet? I've fallen into the same hole in the same road so many times it's time to take a new road. Amen. So we have to let it go. Forget about it. Empty it out like a child, a newborn. Fresh start. What God is saying to me, to us, more than ever before is, "My kids, my children, you're strong to me with your mouth open or closed. You're strong to me to strengthen my church because of the relationship we have to each other. If you keep this relationship as strong as you can, treasure it above all things. 'I will be as effective in you as you will allow me to be a Father to you to hold you, to love you.'" God wants us, He needs us. We need to be more His children. He needs us. We need to be more in love with Jesus. And also to be joyful, truly joyful in His choice of Him choosing me and you. God said do this and I will use you. Read 2 Corinthians 6:18 in the Bible.

Up until now I know it was always me that slowed down the process God had for me. My best thinking has gotten me right to here. My ideas, my ways of doing things kept me sick longer. My best figuring, conniving, manipulating and cons have only helped deny me what God wanted for me all along. So many things I could have enjoyed if I didn't tie it all up with my own issues. Get it? But today, I see the true vision God is beginning to show me and why He's been telling me all along to rest, to let it all go. To trust totally in Him. Oh how simple.

Ain't no valley high enough. Ain't no valley low enough. No bondage too strong. No sin too bad. No pain too hard. Nothing on earth too awesome that can keep you from God if you don't want it to. Don't look back. Forgive and forget the past. Look up and not down. Look forward.

There is no more important work on the face of the earth than the work of intercession. Isn't that what God gave Jesus to do?

As Jesus grew in age and wisdom, He grew in the knowledge of God's love. So get little like a child so God can love you with a father's love. A father's caring. We can begin to learn more and understand this by our own experiences with our children. What it is to love with a father's heart.

It's That Simple. It's the Same Thing. We Make it More Difficult

How I made it more difficult for myself started with the fact that when I was seven years old my father left me, my mom and three older sisters. So first, what did I know or learn about a father's love? And second, I was left as the only man in the family, at seven years old. And now where was I supposed to go to learn how to be a man? You see learned behaviors, which can be good or bad, become a part of us as we try to learn and mature. It's where we learn and from whom that molds us and shapes us into who and what we become. So if you learn how to be a man or woman in all the wrong places you may need to go through some turmoil and pain to relearn, rethink and change some learned beliefs and get it right.

Needless to say, a lot of my early education came from many of the wrong places. In the streets. In the pool halls, nightlife, nightclubs, party people, jail and prison. This is where I started to learn to be a man. Even though I've gotten some unbelievably strong learning experiences from the above places, I had to rethink and relearn a lot resulting in a lot of pain, which in turn has now brought me to this place. Amen. You know I could go on forever on some of the experiences I went through in these last few paragraphs alone. I could write a few books just on that. I would probably make some money off these kinds of books. But today, for me, that's not what it is all about.

It's not about how much money you make. It's about how much difference you make in someone's life.

In short, what I'm saying here, and what God needs us to help Him do in us, is to clean up what we messed up and start our lives sort of all over again. Get little like a child again. "God, my way doesn't work so good. I need a better way." Now don't get me wrong. We learn and we grow from all of life's ups and downs. We gain some true wisdom and knowledge from it so we don't change as much as we acquire more, right? In all things we get a little more experience. A little more wisdom. Hopefully good wisdom, but we keep growing one way or another. So when I say become like a child I am talking about letting go of old learned behaviors and beliefs, and it's an action step in trusting. Trusting the way you did when you were a child. Trusting first that God is cleaning up our hearts. Our minds. Our spirits. Our bodies. He is letting go of certain stuff (fasting), and turning away more from our desires of the flesh. Turning more completely to God's desires. Don't forget when I talked about the things that kept me sick longer, it's the same thing here. It's the things we hold on to that are holding us back. It's time to flip the script so to speak. No matter how educated we are, we must become like a child. In our thoughts there will come this new revelation of how simple it all really is. Instead of saying, "When I was young or little, I used to think…" Now we need to say, "When I was big, I learned to think…" Get it?

Keep it simple stupid

As we become little and low we learn to listen to our hearts. God speaks to our hearts. We need to understand this point. God speaks to our hearts. Don't be in such a hurry. We need to make sure something is from God before we do it. When you were a child, did you ever play the game where you stood in front of a classmate and then had to close your eyes and fall backwards and hope that the person you stood in front of would catch you under the arms so you would not crash your butt on the ground? This was a game to learn trust. Something outside of yourself, right? Same thing, but now we play it with God. When you hear His order then do it. Then it's God's move. Then it's my move. I don't have to fully understand it all. I don't have to be on top of everything. As long as God's winning and we're getting more sensitive to Him, then we are winning too. He wants us to be faithful like this to His every call, big or small. In sickness or in health. As all prophets, healers, and miracle workers before us were faithful so we must be. God can and will only use us when we are low. Little before Him. When we start to get big again, that's when we will screw up. When we start to live our own ideas and plans, that's where we will screw up. So we, as I have now realized, must let go of the need to have it all figured out. God's got it figured out. God knows exactly what, where, when and how He wants to do it all. So let Him. And let's not get discouraged when God gives you a taste, then He backs off a bit. I believe this is His way of not overwhelming us, and also so we stay focused on the true power source. But be absolutely assured that as we remain totally dependent on God when we need the power, the anointing, it will always be there on time.

Open Up

Pain = gain. Gain = motivation. Motivation = understanding. Understanding = surrendering myself. Surrendering self allows God ways to be in you and being in you allows God's ways to go through you.

Remember the pipe illustration in the first part of this book where as children we start with a clean slate. It would look like this.

But as we grow more into ourselves, we start corroding the pipe up with our sinful nature, so it looks like this.

← Corroded with pride, fear, lust, and greed.

Now we have stopped God from flowing smoothly through to us. Same principle, just a little more depth in its understanding. So as we surrender, open and clean up and show our full, true selves to God and others then God can use us in a mighty way.

My God. Even as a small part of the big picture God has in store all I can say is "My God. Wow." So in keeping ourselves little and surrendering all our self-issues and opening up to our true inner beings, then God will say:

"You want security? My little child, I'm your security."

"I have started this good works in you and I will complete that work."

"You want understanding? I'm all understanding."

"You look for peace? I'm the fullness of peace."

As we move forward with God and He is now using us in His plan, isn't that healing in itself? God just using a broken, sinful person in bondage like me is a healing miracle all by itself. With God's healing grace, with God using us and as we truly come to know who's flowing through us like the pipe, in each new revelation after revelation we see and feel His love. As long as we can stay humble and keep ourselves little, He will use all of us in His plans and He will protect all of us and surely guard us from any possible harm. Isn't that pretty easy to get? If it is God's plan there's no way He's going to let anyone destroy or interfere with His plan.

So if He's using us then nothing and nobody can stop Him or us. And also understand that God has spoken to us and all He has promised will come to pass. It has to for how can this mighty powerful religious being go back on His word? Impossible. As we now have opened up to Him, reached out, cried out hopeless, beaten, willing, He will see in us all this true desire. The desire that through it all we still have done our best to be faithful. So little by little He will help us and scrape out the debris we have corroded in the pipes so we can be faithful or can continue to be faithful as this process of growth into the calling is achieved. He has and will continue to use all the circumstances we have spoken about in this book. The death, the abuse, the pain and suffering in our lives to grant within all of us the true blessings He has always had in store for us. That's the Father's love. Amen.

Seven Gifts of the Spirit

Briefly, I want to share with you seven gifts of the Holy Spirit. These gifts, and I said gifts, from God to us are meant to give us the power to strengthen us and to help us restore in ourselves and others God's intentions from the start.

1. Wisdom. The absolute ability to use what we have already learned and to not only use it but to do so when and in the right place and time for the right purpose. The purpose God intended it to be used from the start. The misuse of this wisdom is what has hindered our progress and growth and has ripped us off from the original benefits we rightly would receive from God if used correctly.

2. Understanding. This is when we begin to fully understand and comprehend what we have first accepted in faith. It allows or awakens us to see the true meaning of what has been revealed to us. Faith is like that car that is driving faster than the others. Understanding is knowing the principles of why it's faster than the rest. Of course, with this type of deeper knowledge we'll get more confident and move on to a far deeper level. The deeper level God wants us to get to.

3. Counsel. This is to know right from wrong. To do the right thing in all kinds of situations. It's an ability to hear God speak to us and guide us. It's not like what I've done with trial and errors. Counsel makes us know and see clearly where we're headed. Guides us even in and through the pain and sufferings, dead ends, mistakes and bad choices and brings us to our full selves.

4. Fortitude. This is the courage to go on and do what's right no matter the consequences. Be it pain, suffering, fatigue, discomfort, ridicule, prison, criticism, or doing what's unpopular, it helps us to deal with all hardships out of the true love God has given to us, strengthens us and protects us in that love.

5. Knowledge. Not like the knowledge in studying or in experience but a spiritual knowledge and perspective. As we begin to see life through the eyes of God with all the glory, beauty and divine order leading us to love, as was originally intended.

6. Piety/Love. This is to see God as our Father and to begin the process of fully understanding His incomprehensible, unbelievable and overwhelming love for us. It makes all a reality obtainable and it helps move us so we can share this love with others.

7. Reverence. This is the true ability to really see God for who God is. To have a deep intensive humbling knowledge of His ultimate greatness. This helps us to begin and to grow in a deep felt true relationship with God. Always aware of His presence and His power and aware that all things and all others and all creations are His.

See Isaiah 11:1-2.

Let me just say as we continue, I now know and want to share with you that we are all made for greater things. I'm just now starting to get this. A higher destiny with God and with each other. Faith, hope and love are only the beginning to help us overcome sin and to help us overcome temptations. And to get us through the corruptions and through the normal little trials of our lives and the higher ones as I tried to share with you on earlier pages of this book.

Now these seven gifts begin to help restore our inheritance that God, our Father has always intended for us. But know this. These gifts, and some more points I will share with you as we continue, are of absolutely no use to you unless or until we all decide to use them. You see it's just this simple. Once again, the essence of true love is that it cannot be forced or manipulated or coerced. A free gift and an invitation to share. The choice is ours to make.

Simply put, we cannot love unless we are free not to love.

Here are a few stories from the Bible to make this point a little clearer. One of our biggest mistakes is the false learned beliefs that is instilled in us since we began which is that we need a lot to get something changed, corrected or done. What can one man or woman do in this great big world? We learn to believe that a lot more can get accomplished if we have a lot of money, a lot of talented people around us and great minds at work. But guess what, none of this matters to God either. As in the Bible again, God uses the least of what one would think is the right people for the job.

In the first part of this book, I gave some examples from the Bible of backgrounds of some of the most mentioned people that God used. The examples included a murderer and thieves. Now please refer to Judges 3:31, which tells the story of a man many of us have never heard of in the Bible. His name is Shamgar. He struck down 600 Philistines with nothing more than an ox goad. An ox goad is a strong eight foot stick used to prod oxen when pulling a plow. His heroic actions led to peace in Israel. This was an unbelievable victory using nothing more than a stick all by himself.

See Exodus 4:1, 9-17. Here is where God used Moses (asked Moses I should say) to lead the people of Israel out of Egypt. Moses was totally afraid of course. One, the people wouldn't listen to him or they would not follow him by himself. So then God said, "Moses, what's that in your hand?" (4:2). Moses replied that it was a walking stick. Moses had to convince the people to follow him. He used it to turn the Nile River into blood. He used it to bring the plagues on Egypt. He used it to part the Red Sea and to perform many miracles in the wilderness. So here it's clear that we see again what God can and will do with any type of person with also very little. Moses' walking stick and Shamgar's prodding stick. When dedicated to God's work they became mighty tools. You see God can and will use what little we have to do great things when we surrender to Him. God is not looking for people with great abilities but for those people who are totally dedicated to following and obeying Him.

Less is more and little is much when God is in it.

If and when we use the little we have to serve our God with all our hearts we all will continue to find out that He will do great things through us when we do our part.

Surrender

Do we not want more life? Do we not want more truth? Do we not want more love? From God? If your answer is yes, then it requires a total yielding of our mind's own intelligence, or total yielding of thoughts of our past. A yielding of our desires for the present and a yielding for our future. In doing this and in trusting in this total surrender, we allow God to use us more, to flow through us more easily and then we start to become more Jesus-like. Here are a few signs to prove I know what I'm talking about as we mature, as we grow closer to God. Don't you now find yourself quieter, more humble? More at rest, peace. You are, as we become emptied of ourselves and more like Jesus. God steps into us more and He becomes more active within us. So we get more passive. God gets more active. Nothing new here. God's been doing this for all of time. Just look at all the saints that are with God already. Since the beginning God has and will continue to hold us in His love and He will not ever let us fail. So we need to surrender. I give up. God help me. I can't do it on my own. I need you God. God help me. God help us all.

To trust fully and unconditionally as a young child. When we fully break it down to this place God can now work and begin through us all. If we only practice this.

Love Him with your whole heart and He will surely fill your heart far surpassing anything you could ever dream of.

Love Him with all your soul and He will surely fill your soul with a new found joy and glowing radiance that you ever could dream of.

Love Him with your whole mind and He will surely change or renew your mind with a mind that's the same as in Jesus.

Please trust me here. God has given this to me and I'm now trying to pass it forward to all of you. This, if applied fully as described is true. All you have to do is come to the Lord and trust. Not 50% of your total selves. Not 75% or even 99.9%. You see that very tenth of a percent will prevent this. God wants 100% to get 100% in return. So we're not just talking about compliance here. There's a big difference between compliance and surrender. To comply is like you're going along to fit in, or to be accepted and then get something for your compliance. Like if I admit my boss is always right then maybe I'll get a raise. So I'll just go along with him so I get the raise.

But surrendering. Now this is a different animal altogether. It's like the difference between admitting and accepting. For example, admitting to someone that you love them. You can say I love you a hundred times and not mean it. But when you accept the fact that you love then that takes on a different total meaning altogether, right? Accepting requires action. Remember I talked briefly in the earlier part of this book when I got down on my knees in the street in 1993. I had over $5,000 on me, a bagful of cocaine, a brand new car, yet I was totally out of my mind and out of control on drugs. So I got out of the car, knelt down in the middle of the street and cried out, "God Help Me." Within ½ block after I had gotten back into the car I was surrounded by at least nine or ten cop cars. So I'm sure God intervened here for me and got some of my attention.

But as I look back today, even though I believe it was at this time I became a new Christian, I wasn't really ready to give up everything. I just wanted God to take away the pain. But I was not ready to do anything close to what was required to make this possible. Get it? Nowhere near 100%.

> *Important Question to ask yourself:*
> *Are you running to God or are you running away from the world?*

So we surrender all we can. Turn it all over to God. What we see and think we see. Surrender our thoughts, surrender our beliefs and our hearts. Our love. Surrender in prayer as we pray. Surrender our lives. Our wills. Then it will begin. God will start to take over a little at a time. His thought will be put into our minds and His words will start to come out of our mouths. As we go, don't think we won't still make some errors as before. But as we take a regular inventory we'll start to see a very big difference. Actually others will see the big difference within us at first even before we do. That's how we know we're on the right track. Also when we're wrong properly admit it and repent it as soon as possible. This very God can keep emptying us out and purifying us a little more at a time until we reach this oneness.

Gifts of Love

Among the many gifts of the Holy Spirit, here are twelve more:

Love, joy, peace, patience, kindness, goodness, generosity, faithfulness, modesty, gentleness, self-control and chastity. These signs or effects are how we can confirm the positive good qualities which will come into all our lives when we begin to exercise all the things we're discussing in this book. Not fear, not doubt, not pain and suffering but the true inheritance that is and was always intended for us from God our Father.

See Galatians 5:22-23.

Good Suffering

Oh I have had oh so many pains and sorrows

Oh and I have lost all my hopes for the tomorrows

And yes, there's been oh so many times when I didn't know right from wrong.

Yet in every situation, especially the bad, God used them to only make me strong.

I've been coast to coast, a lot of places.

Been there, done that, seen so many faces.

Been in a stadium of screeching fans, cheering at me yet still feeling all alone.

Yet in those many, many, many a lonely hours, God, Jesus and the Holy Spirit let me know I was their own.

So now I praise God for the great times and for all the hell He's brought me through too

Because if I never had any problems I wouldn't know He would solve them, or what faith in Him can do.

Author: Frank (2012)

We have over one hundred billion brain cells and 60,000 miles of blood vessels in the average child and about 100,000 in the average adult. This is according to the popular internet website webmd.com. The study of DNA has taught us that we are realizing how complicated and complex we truly are. God who can and did create us is able to recreate parts or all of us as He chooses out of one simple thing. Freely out of love. Each day brings with it a new beginning or a new start. A fresh start to be more emptied. Be more open. Be more filled. He can and will only fill a person that is emptied. So as we accept the beauty of brokenness now we can know a new joy of wholeness.

Purified, transformed. I surrender God. From the time I met my girlfriend Judy she could choose a better path for me then I could for myself. So why did I make this all so hard at first? Amen.

Love's Magic

Love can't be seen yet it is the most beautiful thing on earth. It's an art.

Love can't be heard and yet it sings the most wonderful sweet songs from the start.

Love can't be measured, only treasured and always in the heart.

Let Go. Let God.

Whatever does not fit in this new life as you come back again and again, let it go. Let go of it. Be content in God's love. Rest in God's love. Let yourself be tuned into God's love and your life will be new and improved. We are transformed. We really don't need to understand it all. We really only need to say always, forever, with an ongoing yes. Let it be. So be it.

> *"Let it be, let it be, let it be, yeah let it be.*
> *Oh, there will be an answer. Let it be."*
> *Excerpt from song,* <u>Let It Be</u>
> *Written by Paul McCartney and John Lennon*
> *Performed by The Beatles*

God's love sure does always seem to come up a lot, doesn't it? It's truly what it's all about. The only really true, creative, everlasting and most powerful force in the entire world is the power of love. It is the deepest power and if you start to practice its applications with this, your stronger faith in God, wow. Watch out for it can and will help us calm every single obstacle in life and more.

So with this new heart and trust of a child, God will take us to a new want or desire in us. A new hunger that will make us all open and empty enough so now He can begin to fill us up His way. So I ask you now as I ask myself often. What am I still holding onto that's preventing God from moving 100% into my life? Whatever it is I need to be rid of it, don't you think? It's that simple.

The Bible says and God asks us to begin to be more Jesus-like. My friend. My brother Jesus? That means I have to begin to love my enemies, right? Well now it starts to get a little warm in here again, doesn't it? This is a very tall order.

Remember Peter walking on the water with Jesus? Then he sank because of fear and doubt. Jesus was right there with him, and still Peter had fear and doubt. I used to think, "Man, if Jesus was right there with me I would do a whole Cha Cha routine on the water." Well, now I'm not as confident because if I truly have faith then isn't Jesus with us all right now, as I write this? As we speak? Sure. Maybe not physically but still with us all nonetheless. My point is there still is a lot of growing to do and it isn't so much about what we all still have to do, as much as it is about stopping God from getting more active in us. Let go. Let God. Let it be.

Circumstances

In the first part of this book, I introduced you to the lifeline continuum I developed that illustrates the high and low points of our lives. This can be done in months and years from birth going forward. See the Agape Love Chapter in Book 2.

I tried to explain that if we stick to God's plan we would get to where God wanted us to be faster because we stay closer to the line. The highs aren't as great perhaps but also the lows aren't as bad either. So we get further faster, right? Let's take this line of thinking further and in the chapters to come. I promise you will begin to understand its importance and how it can and will change the world if we choose to apply it. It's so simple.

I've developed most of this on an individual level in an attempt to get to know myself better and to try to figure out why I was doing the things I was. And then I realized that I was for the most part my own worst enemy. My inability to respond to some of life's terms in a smooth and appropriate manner. Sure I took some very hard hits in life, but in all honesty, my ways of dealing with them kept me sick and hurting a lot longer than it had to. As I review all this, I feel this is all of us in a nutshell. This is exactly what we as a society have been doing wrong and I mean wrong since time began. We have not and do not learn from our elders anywhere close to the way we should. Don't worry I will prove all this to you. We don't learn from our mistakes. We, as a society, keep repeating the same mistake over and over. For some reason we think we're going to get different results than we have been getting for centuries. But guess what? We won't.

As an individual, I used to overthink everything. I would over intellectualize, which according to the dictionary, means I would analyze something to the extreme. And this kept me sick longer because I couldn't accept someone else's way of doing things even when it seemed to work for them. As a society, as a whole, we do the same thing. Example: there are so many different religions and expert theologians representing all of them and debating on this and that doctrine or what a particular scripture means, and who's right or wrong. Guess what? With everyone continuously doing this our world and the people in it have stayed stuck in the same place for longer than we need to. We're not sharing our knowledge. We're not learning from our mistakes. Everyone thinks they are right.

We could pay it forward. Pass it on from generation to generation. Like a relay race, the runner doesn't start over just to keep making the same mistakes or waste the same amount of time over and over again. Each runner does his or her part and then passes the baton where they left off to the next person. So finally the race is completed as it should be, right?

We will get right back to this thought or revelation but let me just add a thought about the highs and lows in our lives and what they are all about and what it all seems to mean as we move forward as individuals and as a people.

> *"Freedom's just another word for nothing left to lose.*
> *Nothing don't mean nothing honey if it ain't free, not now."*
> *Excerpt from song, <u>Me and Bobby McGee</u>*
> *Written by Kris Kristofferson and Fred Foster.*
> *Performed by Janis Joplin*

Have you tried to make a lifeline on yourself yet? Try it.

I've come to realize that the choices we make has a direct effect on where we come from and where we are today. I've now come to the realization that God in His own way and in His own time will move when the time is right. In His time, not ours.

You see we all tend to think that when we're doing good God is pleased and will do more of what we ask Him, right? Well, you know when I look at some of the most powerful and profound times God moved in my life or worked with me and for me it was at some very low points. Remember I told you about the time I was high on cocaine in the street. Some people, street people, worldly people would say if you had more than $5000 in your wallet, a new car and a bagful of cocaine, well, that wasn't a low. After I knelt down in the street and called out to God in prayer to help me, He moved right then and there. Yes it was a low point. I was lost in sin, weak and alone.

Another time I was in a correctional facility and God moved in my life. And don't laugh but one time I was on the toilet smoking a cigarette and drinking a cup of coffee and guess what? God showed me a vision right then and there. So my point is, it's never what we do or it's never what we've earned. It's not in our understandings or on our time tables. It's all on His. So now again why do we have pain and sufferings in this life? I'm sure sometimes God needs them to get more of our full attention, don't you think? I also now seem to understand that the more responsible we become, the freer we are. Don't forget once again it isn't so much what we all have to do so much as what we all have to stop doing. Then God can be active within us all and move as He deems appropriate for us as a people. The more responsible as individuals we become as a people, the freer we are as individuals, as people, as individuals, as one.

One thought. His thought.

One word. His word.

One power. His power.

One energy. His energy.

One mind. His mind.

One spirit. His spirit.

One plan. His plan.

One love.

And God has promised us all we will be one and so we can stop looking for approval or for false confirmations from other people that we're great or okay. And we need not get approval from others or our own approval that we're on the right path.

Our God will, I promise you all, provide these assurances in the most unexpected times when we all least expect them. God just wants our trust. He's in control. He has any and all power to fix, change or correct every situation. He just wants our focus on Him and not on the situation. Let me say this again. He just wants our focus on Him and not the situation. We are now learning the power and the authority of His love, so don't ever give up or lose your heart. Jesus has been praying for over 2000 years that we all may be one as He is one with God. So what do you think? We won't be one with Him? I promise you; how can we doubt it? We will be one. Amen.

Child of a Deathless Morn
You were not ever born
You will not ever die
For time is mind's ancient lie
Its fleeting fancy's pass
Across minds looking glass
Forever old and new
No child of time are you.
But through eternity you are and will be
And have the meaning whole
Already in your soul.

Author: Frank (1979)

God's Waiting for Us

No one can truly be yours until you're willing to set the person free. And no one can make a free choice unless you give them that choice to make.

So then now does God cause or initiate all the pain and suffering? Absolutely not. A lot of people will argue this but again I say absolutely not. It's because He does give us all free will and freedom of choice. Remember World War I and World War II? Remember Vietnam, Adolf Hitler, Charles Manson, Jeffrey Dahmer, Osama Bin Laden, Ed Gein? Unfortunately, more names and events could be added to this list to make my point.

Why then do these people victimize good people? Why do people victimize other people in general each and every day? Another reason I'm sure is because God can't just stop it without taking away our inheritance of free will and free choice. This is the freedom that makes us human and the freedom that eventually makes us true to Him. As humans we have hurt, cheated and stolen from each other. We have abused, robbed and destroyed each other and so we are the ones responsible for the pain and suffering, right? Not God. Us. There is no other way to explain or justify all the evil.

Another aspect of pain and suffering we all have to deal with is that which is caused by a force outside of us and that is an act of nature. Hurricanes, tidal waves, earthquakes, volcanoes, tornadoes and other natural disasters. We have no power or total control over any of it. These and more, yet they do cause us a lot of pain and suffering. And here is another example of our stupidity. Our government, Corporate America and the major insurance companies refer to these conditions as Acts of God. Remember we talked about learned beliefs. Guess what? These are not Acts of God. These are Acts of Nature.

So now we begin to see a little deeper. God is not blind. God is fair. God is compassion. God is justice. God is forgiving. God is love. God didn't cause the floods deliberately – well maybe the Red Sea, but in all generality, He didn't do it to cause His people pain. The difference between an Act of God and an Act of Nature is His act is when we all come together after the flood and love and help each and every one through it.

Airplane crashes, car accidents, house fires, electrical fires, collapsed bridges or buildings – I believe these things that also cause pain are due to man-made errors or lack of abilities to make things that can work or last forever. If things wear out or fall apart it is because man made it, not God. Again, a lot of unanswered pain, hurt and suffering coming from our own doings, not God's. So now the big question should also lead to this. Not only asking why does God allow all the pain and suffering? But why do we cause so much pain and suffering? And what do we do about it? About all the pain now that it's here.

Isn't pain also a warning sign that something is wrong?

Don't you for a second get me wrong here. I believe without a doubt that God can do whatever, whenever, anytime to anything. Yet there are things in place that must fit in to His total plans for the world. For all of us. I do believe in all miracles in the past and also those that are happening today. And I know God is creating miracles in our lives, in my life as we speak, as I write this. God did divide the Red Sea so the Jews could cross it. God did send the rains to answer one righteous person's prayer. God can change the course or currents of the rivers, or move the sun around, even going backwards in the sky above. The healings. The raising of the dead. Walking on water. How about when the walls of Jericho all crashed down at once? Seven miles of wall at once, or when Paul was in prison and all the chains fell off the prisoners and all the doors unlocked at the same time? Or when David defeated Goliath? Or when Meshach, Abednego and Shadrach survived the fiery furnace unscathed? You see, God can and will provide what is needed when it is needed and is doing so each and every day. No doubt about this.

Pain ignored or pain as a warning sign. Think about an athlete who ignores the pain in his or her knee or the runner who ignores the pain in his or her knee. Both taking a drug to ease the pain only to have to prematurely end their careers. What about other athletes who suffer crippling injuries permanently because they forced themselves to ignore pain or they take drugs that would stop the hurt and pain? Think of all who had been rushed to emergency rooms around the world because they minimized the realities of mild pains thinking it would just go away. We feel pain when we pull muscles. We feel pain when we get too close to a flame. So again we feel pain not as a way of being punished by God but as a warning.

Suffering came into the world because of human sinfulness and God uses it in various ways.

Perhaps you were young and suffered some abuses as so many have. Emotional, physical, or sexual. Perhaps you were beaten up by adults in an abusive manner or slapped or hit by a parent, sibling, or other relative. Perhaps you were abused by church officials or counselors. This, of course, would lead us all, as it did me, to another learned belief, that all unpleasant things that enter into our lives are painful punishments. Again, this is all man-made is it not? There's also a flipside to this. As horrible as what I just referred to is, the reality is it is very hard to appreciate a beautiful sunset when you have a bad toothache. Still, life as we know it would not only be dangerous it would ultimately be unlivable if we did not have pain and suffering. "I lift mine eyes to the hills, from where does my help come? My help comes from the Lord" (Psalm 121:1-2). It does not say in this scripture that my pain comes from God or from the Lord. It's clear it says my "help" comes from the Lord.

Psalm 23

The Lord is my Shepherd; I shall not want.

He maketh me to lie down in green pastures: He leadeth me beside the still waters.

He restoreth my soul: He leadeth me in the paths of righteousness for His name's sake.

Yea though I walk through the valley of the shadow of death, I will fear no evil. For thou art with me. Thy rod and thy staff they comfort me.

Thou prepares a table before me in the presence of mine enemies: thou anointest my head with oil; my cup runneth over.

Surely goodness and mercy shall follow me all the days of my life; and I will dwell in the house of the Lord forever.

So now back to the basic theme here and again let's add just a little more on to this problem/solution. One more thing that has happened to me when I have been hurt by life is I always seemed to have a tendency to hurt myself even more. Have you ever done this? I did this and more. I would view anything bad that happened to me as a direct attack on me because I was a bad person and somehow deserved the crap that was happening to me. I also would push away anyone who would or could be of aid or help. I've always been good at self-destruction. How about you? Do you find yourself guilty of any of this? Are you a victim of abuse, violence, rejection, abandonment or injury? Did this life on life's terms of pain and confusion make us all not only drive people away and alienate us from others, but also run from the realities of it? I was always very good at running from my pain. I ran from relationships. I ran from any long term responsible life choices and I learned how to do drugs and party. I chose jobs and a career that would make the partying lifestyle even easier and guess what? Isn't using drugs a form of running? Running from emotional pain and suffering is running from myself.

If Heaven or the Kingdom we seek is God's, then the way to get there has to be God's. Who else's? Any other way or means has to fail.

So I let myself self-destruct and continued to do the wrong thing because I somehow believed that just getting high and not dealing with any of the truth was easier than dealing with the pain. I gave in to the pain of guilt, shame, anger, resentment and jealousy and added self-imposed loneliness which made my bad situations even worse. Have you done this too?

Back to the point of who causes the pain and why and how we keep ourselves sicker and the pain and sufferings much longer than we have to. Isn't this why we as a society have not progressed as we should have?

Let me just add this so I don't mislead anyone. Some believe God allows suffering and pain to teach us compassion. Others believe we suffer for past bad actions (sins), even sins from a previous life.

Yet I believe none of these truly fit with the God of my understanding and the God that's clearly described in the Bible. These responses indicate or suggest that

God is not in any way affected by our pain. That would first contradict all the good healings and miracles God performed through Jesus to heal the sick and raise the dead so why would He do something to make it harder for us to love Him. He would not. And God is not a cruel God clearly. So if we look closer at what we're taught in the Bible, we'll see and maybe we should all be thankful that God is a patient God. I know I am thankful. No, He is not testing us either. God can't and won't be tested by evil or use evil to test us. See James 1:13. Don't forget God's primary attribute is love. See John 4:8. God is portrayed as a loving, caring parent in Isaiah 49:15. God does not cause people to suffer. See Genesis 18:25.

Yet people are suffering and in pain all the time. Back to God being patient and why I'm grateful for it. I believe God allows free choice for us and allows us time to make our decisions and free choices. If He would have judged me for all my bad choices and sins as they happened or occurred, I would have been in Hell a long time ago. So He does allow the suffering people cause to other people. Suffering that the manipulation of the devil caused us to do.

Yet He is waiting because He does not desire any of us to be destroyed by our sin. He wants us all to repent. His patience again for us here is more proof of His love, and His mercy for all of us. Now can He wipe out the pain? Of course. The suffering? Yes. All the bad people, tyrants, terrorists and murderers who are unwilling to change their evil ways? Yes and He will have to destroy such people soon. See 2 Thessalonians 1:6-9.

<u>So it's simple. Repent. I almost have to repent daily. Do you? It's childishly simple. Exactly.</u>

Therefore, let us all start to add to all our prayers for determination, willpower and the power to do instead of just pray. To become instead of just wish. Amen.

More Control

Four steps to help us to control and govern ourselves:

1. Prudence, which is the habit of focusing on the true good in every circumstance and choosing the right means to achieve the true good.

2. Justice, which is the habit of respecting the rights of others and God in every circumstance.

3. Temperance, which is the habit of mastering our instincts and keeping our desires within the limits of what is honorable in every circumstance.

4. Fortitude, which is the habit of constantly pursuing what is good in every circumstance despite facing difficulties, temptations and obstacles.

Talk about some tall orders? But is it really, if we think about it? Didn't we say the more we surrender to someone else's way (God's plan) the more we turn it all over? Let it go. Get little and trust in the power greater than ours. Also, remember in the first part of this book, I talked about saying the word *no* enough times that it becomes a habit. The same thing applies here. Acting right is just as much a habit as acting wrong. Learned behaviors are like learned beliefs. If we learn them we can unlearn them by practicing something different and do the something different so much that we fake it until we make it.

Again, say yes or no enough times until it becomes a habit. I talk about this because it worked for me some years ago. I was working hard as a manager at a car dealership. I also ran a coffee club on the side and for some reason, I stayed away from drugs using this simple practice of saying no. I didn't smoke cigarettes or drink or do anything for almost five years straight after, mind you, being heavily addicted to drugs. Five years and it started by me just practicing no. And it did become a habit. The no was automatic after a time. Also, let's just say here that even though this was a program of my own self-will, I don't believe nothing is for nothing, do you?

God Doesn't Gamble

As we talk a little more about prayer and as we discussed all the miraculous ways God answered some prayers in the past, walking on water, raising the dead and so forth, I would like to bring our attention to a form of what I believe is also a firsthand miracle. I was clean and sober somehow for five years straight with seemingly no help. That was a miracle.

I'm sure this has happened to all of us at one time or another after we hit a traumatic time, and experience the pain we've been talking about, whatever the situation. I know prayers are answered daily and I know we all have experienced this form of miracle. No matter what your life experience was, a death, divorce or some other kind of tragedy, at some point you felt what's the use of going on?

We were all broken to a point of despair. We even got to the point of being incapable of responding, to even continue on with life, the promise of being even alive. But we prayed and others prayed for us and we didn't seem to get the answers we thought we wanted, like returning a loved one or healing a family member of a serious disease. But what did actually happen? Somehow we found the strength to carry on. We did not completely break. We found the fortitude to go on living and start caring about things again, even more so.

So, like so many in the Bible and so many of us today, we all faced simply impossible situations, scary, painful, hurtful situations and we found out we were a lot stronger than we knew we were. As we prayed, as we opened ourselves up to God. Remember, surrender. Let go. Get little. We were a lot stronger and in better shape to handle it all than we ever thought we would be because we opened up our hearts in prayer. We may not have gotten the instant relief or the painful problems to totally disappear or the miracle to totally remove the tragedy, but we all discovered people all around us that were willing to help. We discovered God right beside us and a strength developed within us to help us survive the pain and tragedy. Now I ask you, is this not an answered prayer? Is this not a form of a miracle?

Why God Why?

God, why is there so much hate crime?

When you taught and showed us the good in all men.

God, why is there so much despair?

When you have given us the means to fix up the ghettos and give hope as well.

God, why is there so much disease?

When you have given us great miracles to heal and to cure.

God, why is there so much starvation?

When you have given us the means to feed the world.

God, why is there so much war?

When you made a world where man can find peace.

So now you didn't get what you prayed for, hey?

Why? Because you didn't deserve it.

You didn't get what you prayed for because you didn't pray right or hard enough.

You didn't get what you prayed for because God knows what's best.

You didn't get what you prayed for because God doesn't hear prayers.

You didn't get what you prayed for because there is no God.

Well, BS. I say we all get what we need and what's best for us according to God's perfect plan. We'll get all we thought we wanted and so much more so let go, let God. According to His will we shall all see the kingdom. Now what did you pray for again?

A Miracle

Sigh of relief. Let's see, we have a medical miracle. I was once diagnosed, and my girlfriend Judy can attest to this because a friend of mine wrote to her about it. She was and still is my angel from God and she came running. To this day she is still running for my silly butt. Anyway, I was diagnosed with a liver tumor that was said to be about the size of a buffalo nickel. At the time the doctors wanted to start chemotherapy right away and I said I didn't believe in that. I believe in divine healings and let's just monitor this. I also had some personal reasons to not get prolonged treatments at the time so we monitored it. Guess what? It disappeared. The doctors said it disappeared. That it was gone. The doctor said he didn't understand it and I told him that I was starting to. He called it a medical miracle.

Of course, now my big brain who likes to overthink wanted to find out more about this cancer of the liver. I learned how serious it can be. Of course there is always a chance for a miracle and medicine for the possibility of a remission. At least until the disease has grown to the point of destruction of the infected area. The bottom line is we can't predict medical miracles. We can't induce them and in the case of this liver stuff, it is unheard of. So I ask you, is this a miracle of man or a medical miracle or what?

Miracles Through Man

Personally it very well might be sacrilegious to let someone die without doing everything possible. Maybe even everything impossible to save the person. If that takes a miracle let's make it happen. Wait a minute. How do we do that? They all talk as if miracles were of a supernatural nature beyond our human understanding. Let me tell you I'm not a big mystical kind of guy. I am, however a hard-headed Greek/Italian man and I can guarantee you that I have seen miracles. How about smoking a joint back when I was in high school, at the lakefront looking up at the moon and then not long after that realizing and then seeing with those same eyes, men walking on that very same moon. You might say that was a miracle.

Also back in school we used to love biology class for many reasons. I remember we studied atoms and also at that time nobody even thought that if we just split this atom thing what would happen? Yet someone did, giving way to unbelievable energy, in fact changing the world forever. Yet before this all one would say that would be a miracle, right?

My grandmother, God rest her soul, could not speak a word of English. She came from Italy to live in the small town of Weirton, West Virginia. I'm sure she never thought she would one day look up in the sky over her home on Marland Heights to see an airplane traveling overhead at the speed of sound. One would have said that's a miracle, right? I loved my grandmother then, and still do now.

My sister has polio. She has lived her whole life with one good leg because of it. What a true pleasure and delight, after all she went through, to see her raise three lovely girls. She has always been an inspiration to the family and shows us every day what character, persistence and goodness is all about. The polio vaccine from the 50's and improved over the years has eliminated this threat since 1979 in the United States. Smallpox was eliminated from the world by 1980 because of a vaccine. Aren't these miracles?

So you can all see clearly that I believe that miracles can be made to happen. And I believe miracles come from God. I believe God can and will and does work a lot of miracles through man.

So far now, as we go on we're learning more about serious areas that I believe, and now I'm finally beginning to know how this affected us as a whole. I won't say it has affected us completely negatively because I know all things work out but for the good of God. But I will say these things certainly stunt our growth processes. The one thing is we think too much. We overthink everything. We're all trying to figure out some things we're not even supposed to or can't. That has kept us all stuck in the same place for far too long. Let's continue on with more about the what, who and why of pain and suffering.

John Lennon and Paul McCartney wrote another song, which The Beatles performed, called "Let It Be."

> *"When I find myself in times of trouble*
> *Mother Mary comes to me.*
> *Speaking words of wisdom*
> *Let It Be."*

> *SURRENDER.*
>
> *LET GO. LET GOD.*
>
> *GET LITTLE.*
>
> *KEEP IT SIMPLE STUPID.*

Here's just one more twist to this important dilemna or serious question on all the pain.

This is based on a lot of Bible scriptures that I've read. Like Romans 8:28 which says, "All things work together for good to them that love the Lord."

"And in everything give thanks for this is the will of God in Christ concerning you" (1 Thessalonians 5:18).

Wait a minute here. Doesn't this make it a little clearer? That we're to be more grateful about all things. About everything. Well, if everything is created by God He must allow all things for His specific reasons and it all will work out for the good of us and the good of God. Then what's the problem? Why are we all tripping? So the twist is maybe God just wants us to learn to appreciate Him more; to thank Him more; to trust in Him more; to learn to allow and let Him work in and through us more.

Here's another little example of the twist. As I said earlier in this book. I'm a recovering drug addict and as we now know, addiction is clearly a disease. For all my life, I would wonder why, if there is a God, He would allow people like me to continuously suffer from this disease of addiction. It almost always without a doubt, when I used drugs or relapsed, led to lots of pain and suffering for not only myself but many of those around me. So why God?

Wait a minute here. Let's look at what Jesus said. "Blessed are ye when men shall revile and persecute you and shall say all manner of evil against you falsely for my sake" (Matthew 5:11). And "Rejoice ye in the day and leap for joy, for behold. Your reward is great in heaven, for in the like manner did their fathers unto the prophets" (Luke 6:23).

What is Jesus saying? Isn't He saying give thanks for everything, good or bad? So we are to thank Him for the pain, to surrender ourselves more to His power and will so we can grow in His way for us. So I now must thank Him for all the pain and suffering my addictions caused me and so many others. Now I must not only just say the words but come to truly believe it in my heart. So I began to try, "Thank you God for my addictions. Thank you God for all the pain it has caused for it's all allowed by You for the good of all sooner or later as is Your will. Thank you God."

So here is the breakdown. I now begin to start thinking, as crazy as it sounds, that God allowed my addiction to teach me something. To maybe not only help me but just maybe to also help others. So it was not an accident at all. All the pain and suffering experiences. God had planned it. So I say again. "Thank you God for this addiction as I trust in You to do with me as You will." My conversation with God went like this:

"What would you like me to do with it?"

"Please help and heal me Lord."

"Heal you?"

"Yes, please."

"What about the reasons you're addicted in the first place? What should we do about all that? What about all the abuses as a child? The issues of abandonment and so forth? What about all that? The resentments, the anger?"

I was puzzled and then it hit me all at once. God was saying to forget all of my life's pain and suffering and not focus on that, but focus on what's important. To focus only on Him. God was saying this to me and now to you as well. That if we don't pay attention to all the symptoms of our problems, but pay attention to God instead, He will heal us.

Every time I prayed for help throughout my addiction and truly tried to believe God would just take it away, I always fell a little short because I had always given up when I felt the symptoms resurface or pop back up on me. So, relying on my own strength and power I would get weak and relapse over and over again. Now I know the symptoms mean nothing. What matters is to believe in God and to have faith in what God says to let go and let God. To surrender to His will. To rely on His wisdom, His grace, His mercy, His protection, His power. Not my own. Not your own. His. Amen.

Faith in Him and in His promise is all I needed. All along, it is what we all need. The pain and suffering are learning devices to get us to see His truth. The following scripture will help us see more of this truth. Paul says in Corinthians 12:9-10, "But He said to me, 'My grace is sufficient for you, for my power is made perfect in weakness.' Therefore I will boast all the more gladly about my weaknesses, so that Christ's power may rest on me. That is why, for Christ's sake, I delight in weaknesses, in insults, in hardships, in persecutions, in difficulties. For when I am weak, then I am strong."

You see we believe, in fact, I know I truly believed up until now that infirmities, pain, suffering, etc. were the very things I always hated and believed were unfair. Or that it happened to me because I wasn't good enough. I don't like it when people go against me or when accidents happen and people are wronged seemingly for no reason. I don't like seeing people get hurt or when things all seem to be going wrong. Yet over and over I not only find words in the Bible to acknowledge this, but all through life's total experiences as well. There is a lot of scripture in Psalm referring to this. David said the following in Psalm 30.

"Sing the praises of the lord, you His faithful people
Praise His holy name.
For His anger lasts only a moment
But His favor lasts a lifetime.
Weeping may stay for the night
But rejoicing comes in the morning.

You turned my wailing into dancing.
You removed my sackcloth and clothed me with joy.
That my heart may sing Your praises and not be silent.
Lord my God, I will praise You forever."

(Psalm 30:4-5, 11)

"Be still and know that I am God."

(Psalm 46:10)

Dr. Charles F. Stanley has written much on the subject of a thankful life. He expresses it better than I ever could, so here are his words. The ten benefits of a thankful life:

1. Constantly reminds us that God is always with us. His presence becomes more and more real to us.
2. Encourages us to search for God's purpose even in the midst of our pain.
3. Helps us submit our human will to God's divine will so we have a change of attitude.
4. Reminds us how helpless we are without God in every situation so that our weakness can become His strength.
5. Forms a stronger trust in God in our hearts while we're walking through the valley of dark circumstances.
6. Lends a key to finding joy. That means peace and contentment, not giddiness.
7. Makes a powerful impact on others when they see us triumphing over very difficult circumstances.
8. Directs our thoughts back to God instead of ourselves or our situation.
9. Gives us new spiritual energy in getting our batteries recharged.
10. Removes anxiety and replaces it with indescribable peace.

So maybe we're truly on to something here. Clearly we're not the only ones talking about all of the material in this book. Many others, way smarter than I am, have seen the truth. Thank you God.

In this chapter we'll begin to more fully understand the priorities which we, as humans feel are important vs. perhaps what someone like our God may feel is important.

Man's Law vs. God's Law

In light of such truth consider the following. Whether or not He answers our prayers for healing or deliverance today takes on a far less importance than where we will spend eternity. We must always remember that we don't ever have to die, spiritually. I still believe He performs miracles. I have seen it as we talked about. But still, how can these relatively short-lived experiences compare with incredible closeness with Him forever. Surely we cannot always understand God.

Man's law. Again, first let me elaborate on the point that our best thinking got us to this place. Remember I said earlier on that I now know my intellectualizing kept me sick a lot longer and now I can also see it's one of our biggest problems in society as well. Still we made laws for us to follow. Man-made laws. The Declaration of Independence was drafted in 1776 by Thomas Jefferson and says, "We hold these truths to be self evident. That all men are created equal."

This language was an attempt to describe what it takes to make a truly human environment or society. It also went on to say that, "They are endowed by their Creator with certain inalienable rights that among those are life, liberty and the pursuit of happiness." These rights are for all man, not just some, right? The individual and not society becomes more important. No government should do what we as people can do for ourselves. Things like preserve, respect and promote. We must always remember that the well-being of each and every person must be the first and foremost concern, and that helping one another must also be the common goal. If not, we will fail.

So here come the laws we had to develop to help us achieve all this because it seems we were too weak on our own to get along as people or as nations. When it comes right down to it, due to our lack of understanding and our brilliant intellectualizing, the only thing we have left in common and the only thing we have to rely on is the law. But man's law can be a very poor way to try to unite or bring people together. Why? Because everybody has different wants, needs, beliefs, morals, values and prejudices. Let me go on. Also understand this, that if and when we make a law it is outdated the day it is passed. Laws are often being revised to fix the mistakes previously made. People are still suffering.

Here, we're not dealing with human life as it should be. We're dealing with the moral, ethical, educational, economical or social situations of life with this man-made crap. Laws may be okay for settling arguments between people but man-made law too often leads to a crowded, confused and often corrupt legal sysem. It's not for helping people grow as one together, all people to help forge ahead as we should. So here we are again. We tried with our best thinking and our best thinkers and intellects got us right here. Stuck.

*"Through wisdom a house is built,
And by understanding, it is established."*

(Proverbs 24:3-4)

The best way to keep our kids at home at night is to provide a peaceful, joyful, happy and loving atmosphere, or you can let the air out of their tires.

Don't get me wrong. We do okay for the most part as a whole and yes, we try our best and the system we have in place is probably the best we could come up with at the time it was established. But we must continue to grow to learn, to improve and get better so why don't we? If the common good as it has been brought to our growth process is the amount or sum of our total rations or allotment of our social conditions, this then allows us to reach our true goals or full potential more easily and more fully.

Confusion, corruption and coercion will always have its part to play in society. But it truly is not there that we all must seek the law of progress.

If only. If only. If only. I get it. If only we could all work together for this one common good in this country, hell in all countries. Then what? Wouldn't we then start to get a little closer to what God wanted all along and wouldn't we be closer to what Jesus meant when He told us to, "Love one another as I have loved you" (John 13:34).

I'm no brilliant individual and none of this is more than common sense and truly not rocket science so why do we not get any further? Why do we not make any progress? Maybe we need to stop all the overthinking. Maybe we need to finally grow up, see the light, pass it on. Pass it on to our kids, and grow up as we help our kids grow up. Let it go. Let God. Finally admit we can only control so much yet we're nothing without God. Nothing. His world. His plan. Anything else is irrelevant and guess what? We have learned it will not work. It's all so simple if we all would just surrender to Him. Don't get me wrong. I also need to do a lot more of this too.

Pray for me as I pray for you. All of us together as one surrender to Him. Give up. Let go. Reach out and up to Him. Basically, do it His way. Keep it simple. Trust. Believe. Have faith in Him. We can't figure it all out anyway can we? We've tried now for what – thousands of years?

"For my thoughts are not your thoughts, neither are your ways my ways, saith the Lord.

For as the heavens are higher than the earth, so are my ways higher than your ways, and my thoughts than your thoughts."

(Isaiah 55:8-9)

Easy Does It

It is yours or God's?

Cease striving as you do.

God's actions begin.

Give it to Him all of it. He will take it and do all that needs to be done.

Hunger and thirst for more of God.

He can only fill what is empty.

There's living only as there's dying.

Resurrection only as there is death.

Author: Frank
Friendship Club 1994

"I have given them the glory that you gave me that they may be one as we are one – in them and you in me – so that they may be brought to complete unity. Then the world will know that you sent me and have loved them even as you have loved me.

Father, I want those you have given me to be with me where I am, and to see my glory, the glory you have given me because you loved me before the creation of the world."

(John 17:22-24)

"His master replied, 'Well done good and faithful servant. You have been faithful with a few things; I will put you in charge of many things. Come and share your master's happiness.'"

(Matthew 25:21)

Stay with me on this. If we recognize that Jesus Christ is the son of God and is our greatest spiritual leader outside of God Himself, who clearly worked many miracles throughout His life on earth, and beyond in learning what we have so far, it is becoming clearer that we are to step towards the goal of becoming more like Jesus Himself. Let's proceed carefully now. The truly best example I can find is the Bible that shows how people should live, like to forgive all things, heal the sick, the diseased and perform miracles. Turning pain and suffering into positives as all turn out for the good of God and then naturally all mankind as a whole. Yes, more like Jesus is the goal. Right?

Be careful as I know more now than when I started to make this discovery. That I was, and we all will surely be walking on very dangerous ground here, so be careful and please pay attention. Let's go on. I didn't fully understand it all but I had begun to look at Jesus as someone like me in many ways, or someone I could be like if I worked hard at it. Remember that Satan has so many tricks to fool or confuse us, like using Christians against other Christians or using unimportant symbolism in different religious organizations to divide the people because of their different beliefs or customs, which actually doesn't mean much and takes us away from what is really important, what we should be and what God wants us to be focusing on instead. Get it? So let me go on.

The goal is to become more Christlike. And in trying to do so we have to ask and question God. Why, why God? Let's not forget that also Satan, since the beginning of time, has and still tries to get us to lose sight of the fact that Jesus died for us on the cross and the resurrection. Don't forget Satan also quoted the Bible all the time, even back with Jesus and still today.

As I'm learning and trying to be so smart and spiritual and believe I have all the answers, wherever I was I talked about and believed the miracles of Jesus, and that we can do the same things, like healing ministries, for instance. Then God showed me a lot more in a little time, like this.

"And we know that all things work together for good to them that love God, to them that are the called according to His purpose."

(Romans 8:28)

You see God knows just like He did with Jesus that when all the sin and suffering passed on through Christ Jesus, it would all turn out and come out in the long run as praise, joy, love and victory. The only time God gives Satan any permission to test us is when God Himself sees the great potential in whatever we're going through, and it will always come out for our best interests in the long run. As it all passes through us it will come out a "pure" praise. "Pure" love. "Pure" joy. "Pure" victory.

Wait just a minute. What this all means is that in believing we can be like Jesus we can easily start to believe we are actually worthy or are stronger, actually able to do some of these things on our own. Wrong answer.

God has shown me as I pass it on to you, that through everything we experience, God said to me, "My son, know this for sure and never lose sight of the fact that you never have to worry about anything of this world or anybody, or this world will hurt you or abuse you or rip you off or mistreat you in any way shape or form unless it is my will. Your life is in my hands my son and you can trust me for everything. And as you continue to see me, seek me, and know me in all things, you will now truly appreciate me and thank me for all. Because surely you will see how perfect I have and will work out each and every detail of your life."

So now is when we truly learn to thank God for everything, no matter what, instead of trying always to avoid or finagle ourselves out of difficult situations. We will in fact grow in character, grow in substance and grow more completely as human beings emotionally and spiritually as well. We not only grow through these situations good or bad. More importantly, we also please God as we do.

Now here's the real message everyone, and why I cautioned us earlier to be careful as we become more Christlike. Don't misunderstand me. We are and should strive to become more like Jesus taught us to live, to be. But we have to never forget through it all that it is not our doing. Just know that at this moment and second, God is trying to fill all our hearts with joy and love. Not because of our efforts nor our righteousness or our greatness, or what we may or may not sacrifice. It is all for only one thing and that is believing in the Lord Jesus Christ.

I ask you now. How many opportunities are we going to let pass us by? How much pain will it take? I hope you don't need as much as I did to finally get this.

Imagine this conversation, and that God is asking now,

"My son, can and will you now live more like Jesus did?"

"I would like to say yes."

"But about your sinful thoughts and wishes, are they worthy? Are they pure?"

"I have to say no."

"Would you like them to be?"

"Well, yes Lord."

"Will you then just give it all to me, all your thoughts and desires?"

"Yes Lord I will."

"Now?"

"Yes Lord."

"How about now and forever and ever?"

"Yes."

So as I now get littler than ever before, empty myself even more than before, surrender yet even more than before, let go, let God and then ask Him to use me more, not my words, my deeds, but God's words, God's deeds through me, I screamed, "Help me God. Use me Lord."

Then I saw Jesus come to me in a vision and He said, with the purest look on His face that I've ever seen, "Frankie, I don't want to use you. I want you to use me."

You see people, in our growing process and as we become more spiritually whole, the devil will try to get us to lose focus on the facts which are, and always will be the cross, the blood and the resurrection of Jesus who died for our sins. It isn't us at all. It is Jesus. Jesus in us. The Holy Spirit through us. God's grace. God's mercy. God's power. Not ours.

The secret, the real honest truth is this. Jesus, when He washed the feet of the disciples, when He died for us, wants to give of Himself for us each and every second. Just as thoroughly as He gave of Himself on the cross. We have and can truly give Him nothing. We have nothing without Him and we have nothing to give Him. We can only thank Him, and we can only receive Him.

The secret is not us being more like Christ even though that's cool. The real secret is Jesus Christ in us. Colossians 1:27 says, "To them God has chosen to make known among the Gentiles the glorious riches of this mystery, which is Christ in you, the hope of glory."

Christ is in us, not that we become like Him, but that He lives in us and transforms us from within. Others may look at us and say we appear to be Christlike, but not because we have become more worthy or holy or spiritual or pure. He lives in us. That's the secret. So now from this book and God's word, God promised that we could do all things in Christ. "I also pray that you will understand the incredible greatness of God's power for us who believe Him. This is the same mighty power that raised Christ from the dead and seated Him in the place of honor at God's right hand in the heavenly realms" (Ephesians 1:19-20).

"Now all glory to God, who is able, through his mighty power at work within us, to accomplish infinitely more than we might ask or think" (Ephesians 3:20).

The highest reward for a person's toil is not what they get for it but what they become by it.

Author: John Ruskin

Childlike

We start out pure, God of course having it right at the very beginning. As kids we're purer, we're innocent, we're trusting. Then we start to grow and want and even need, so we then try to decipher sometimes with the help of others, sometimes on our own, what we want and need and then in turn attempt to make the decisions as to what we need or want and what we think is good for us. This is where the mistakes begin and usually snowball into pain, suffering, conflicts, fights, war. I'm sure some of you have made a lot of bad choices based on your desires, mainly of the flesh. The "if it feels good do it" theory.

We see others with something we want, whether physical, emotional or financial. What happens when we don't get it? Our expectations go unfulfilled so we become upset. How upset can depend on a lot of things. But know this, sin is sin. Don't forget God looks at our hearts only. In James 4:1-2, "What causes fights and quarrels among you? Don't they come from your desires that battle within you? You desire but do not have, so you kill. You covet but you cannot get what you want, so you quarrel and fight. You do not have because you do not ask God."

So why the pain and suffering? What then in fact makes us unhappy or mad or depressed, even frustrated, angry or resentful? Why can't we all just get along? And why are we always so pissed off and in panic and so anxious all the time? Why are we not walking in a lot more peace, more joy and contentment? Isn't the answer becoming much more obvious now? For me I know that even if I'm sober today and proclaim to be church-going, even if I'm born again and I'm also baptized in the Holy Spirit, why am I still so depressed, empty, clearly missing something. Why? My point is we can be Christians, believe in Christ (born again), baptized in the Spirit and still be a completely messed up, unhappy, miserable person. So this might begin to show us that even these things, believing in Jesus, being born again, having been baptized in the Holy Spirit, are all absolutely essential for us. There are obviously other things that we all must have to learn and apply within ourselves and within our lives if we are to live a more victorious happy, joyful life here on Earth. One of the most important things is to be totally dependent upon God. The biggest of all this we must learn, as I have to as well is that up until now my relationship with God was based on what I thought I could do. On doing, instead I had to learn to come to Him, humbly in total dependence, instead of trying to be independent and hard-headed and falsely or pretentiously righteous or worthy, because I am not. And as we've seen we truly can't seem to work much of life's issues out on our own. I know I can't work mine out on my own or work things out for myself. Even when I try something within me will block God's flow, will frustrate or counter what's best for all or what I think is best, when only God knows what's best. What's best for all mankind. We have to learn to come to God in total dependence like a little child. How childish. Exactly.

"When I stopped seeing my mother with the eyes of a child she became a whole lot smarter mentally, emotionally and spiritually. And I saw the woman and the angel that helped me give birth to myself."

Author: Nancy Friday

"And the spirit of the Lord shall rest upon him, the spirit of wisdom and understanding, the spirit of counsel and might, the spirit of knowledge and of the fear of the Lord."

(Isaiah 11:2)

Father, may my children fulfill your plan and purpose for their lives.

I Choose Love

Before I became a mentor, a facilitator, an elder and a parent, I had all the answers on how this world and all the people in it could better bring up the children. Now I have only one. Love them, especially when they don't deserve to be loved.

"Be still and know I am God."

(Psalm 46:10)

Faith equals _____.
Grace equals _____.
Yet faith and grace equal everything.

More Kid Stuff

First, faith equals ____. Note faith is not the cost or price that buys God's blessings. The Bible says in Matthew 17:20, "If you have faith the size of a mustard seed you will say to this mountain, 'move from here to there,' and it will move and nothing will be impossible for you."

So with so many good people out here why aren't we moving even a little bit? So now wait a second here. Isn't faith a type of works? I mean here is something we make happen. For example, we can't receive anything by faith alone unless first we ready our hands to grasp it. Correct? Let's not forget, I believe this is very important to our growth and necessary as well. So that's why I've jumped into this, okay? Let me continue. Let's not forget that when we get mad or feel frustrated, it's most likely that we have entered into ourselves own abilities or power. Our "own" efforts. Remember this. Our own efforts, more often than not, left us with pain and suffering. Our own efforts left us weak and powerless so we have to wonder what's going on. This is a bit confusing. What's this faith stuff all about then? Well, I believe this. If faith requires some work on our part then to equal out the crap we mix along with this formula, we have to allow God, or ask God to add to our little faith His grace and we're on to something right?

Grace equals ____. Now through faith is the grace of God brought forth to us. Again faith isn't the prize, it's the means or should I say the vessel for which God's grace can work in and through us. Remember the pipe illustration back in an earlier chapter of this book?

You see my friends God's grace, again not our works or doings, but His grace, His love, makes everything and I mean every pain, suffering, conflict, fight, every war, easy to deal with and overcome. Left alone on our own resources would otherwise seem impossible and unbearable. Jesus said, "For my yoke is easy and my burden is light" (Matthew 11:30). So it is the devil who wants to put this heavy burden crap on us. This burden I spoke of a little earlier is brought on by us, by our fleshly desires or our works of the flesh and our efforts to gain what we think we need. Now am I making a little more sense here?

As a child we know, "Jesus grew and became strong in spirit, filled with wisdom and the grace of God was upon Him" (Luke 2:40). This tells us everything, doesn't it? We don't need all this pain and suffering any more. We don't need all the worldly or flashy things we always thought we needed. We always seem to believe we need something else, something more and that the grass is always greener on the other side. If only I did this or that, or I should have done this. The what-ifs. The coulda, woulda, shoulda.

You see the truth is that to be happy, truly happy, to be filled, healthy, wealthy and wise, prosperous and successful, there is only one thing that we need. And it is the same thing that Jesus needed as well. Here I go again, starting to make sense. We need, as Jesus did, to be emptied of all our self crap, so we can then be filled with God's will. His will, His wisdom and having His grace upon us. There is not a thing on this earth and beyond that we need if we're right and I know we are. I would not share this or speak if I didn't know it to be the absolute truth as it has been given to me. Not intentionally anyway. Amen. So again nothing would, should or could be even remotely impossible for us to do. If God created the world and everything in it, as we know He did. I haven't seen anyone or anything remotely close to explaining it all otherwise anyway. So God created everything. That means the air we breathe, the water we drink and the food we live on. Everything we do, everything we are and everything we have or don't have is by the grace of God.

Yes it's true that we as Christ-like Christians are becoming more Christlike and can do all things through Christ who strengthens us. Yet know this. That it's only true because it is due to the grace of God. "For we are God's handiwork created in Christ Jesus to do good works, which God prepared in advance for us to do" (Ephesians 2:10).

John 15:1-6 tells us, "I am the true vine, and my Father is the gardener. He cuts off every branch in me that bears no fruit while every branch that does bear fruit He prunes so that it will be even more fruitful. You are already clean because of the word I have spoken to you. Remain in me, as I also remain in you. No branch can bear fruit by itself; it must remain in the vine. Neither can you bear fruit unless you remain in me. I am the vine; you are the branches. If you remain in me and I in you, apart from me you can do nothing. If you do not remain in me, you are like a branch that is thrown away and withers, such branches are picked up, thrown in the fire and burned."

It's clear that God laid out our lives and that means our life's work before the world was created. So we can all stop wondering what church is right, what symbol is the right one to use and what sacrifices we need to do this or that. Should we take communion or should Jesus be on the crucifix we wear on our necks? The reality is that it is crystal clear that it is God's ministry. God's church. His works. So instead of bragging of our great power, our new great knowledge and accomplishments, we should just bow down each new morning surrendering to this loving God, saying, "Here I am God. I am as empty as I can get or as much as you taught me how to be so Your will, Your grace can flow in and through me. I can do only what you God allow me to do."

So then if you are like the pipe that we talked about and God works through us guess what my friends? We are now God's partners and if God is in complete control of our life and this world and the world to come, then because we now know all this truth, the stuff that hurts us, the pain, the suffering, all that stuff that seems to go wrong, we cannot be upset or discouraged because we know God is just working out His plan for us. So you see we are becoming more aware that while faith is important, we are learning to commit ourselves more to God, to begin to trust Him more in all things and not relying on our miraculous faith but only on God's miraculous great grace. To repeat, it's not because of anything we do on our own. Not our works or abilities or knowledge. It's because of God's love for us and His willingness and strength to meet each and every one of our needs and at no price to us. He charges us nothing. Not a thing. This is grace. Faith and God's grace equals everything.

It's good for our kids to learn to win and also to learn to lose. This way they will learn that in life there's going to be ups today and maybe downs tomorrow.

How Childish. Exactly.

"Embracing the potent mixture of joy, suffering, brilliance and confusion, that characterizes the human experience. No escape?"

Author: Pema Chodron

The Wisdom of No Escape

Jesus said in Matthew 18:2, "Truly I say to you unless you repent and become like little children you can never enter the kingdom of heaven." Here He was talking of a physical sense. Here now again is Jesus talking about it in a spiritual sense. "Truly I say to you, whoever does not accept and receive and welcome the kingdom of God like a little child shall not in any way enter it" (Luke 18:17).

How can we become more like a child again? Some say kids are stupid or silly or ridiculous. I don't think this is absolutely true. Sure, at times when we're growing up we may have acted stupid or silly. We may have been ridiculous or acted silly. We may have been taught incorrectly or learned some wrong beliefs. But I believe that for the most part children are more trusting, more forgiving and more loving. Let's take a little step back and see if this makes sense. I know as a child, from a broken home who had moved way too much to catch any steady solid guidance, Satan did not waste time figuring out who or what I was to become. He tried to take me out early. My childhood was devoured by sexual, physical, verbal, mental and even emotional abuses. Let's just say that I chose to deal with these strong issues in a very inappropriate manner. Turning to drugs and eventually becoming addicted because of the temporary avenue it provided to take the pain away worked for a short time so I did it. I did a lot of other not so pleasant things to try to fit in or learn what life was about and I did this in all the wrong places. Like the streets, the pool halls, nighclubs, jail, etc. What I'm saying is that the devil tried to take me out when I was gullible and powerless and at a time when I was desperate to gain knowledge and understanding about what life was and how to become a man. The devil jumped at the chance to destroy me. But guess what? I'm still here to talk about it more than 50 years later.

Let me get to the point. I allowed all the BS and negative stuff into my life because I didn't know any better. I was gullible and had to learn everything the hard way. I'm very hard-headed anyway. What's more important here is what God is looking for. What Jesus is talking about, right? God is not looking for the gullible child. He's looking for the trusting child.

It was my true nature to start life trusting everything and everyone. It wasn't until I experienced bad or terrible consequences from these various experiences that I began to learn not to trust at all. Decades of pain and BS followed.

If being a kid meant being bullied all the time, pushed around, abused, taken advantage of and used, I needed to learn how to grow up fast or at least pretend to be grown up. So now a ton of other mistakes began, all symptoms from the first one. Needless to say, it took me way too long to just get to the place I'm at today and God knows I still have a long way to go. But I now believe and know what God, what Jesus, was talking about and trying to teach us. As we discussed in earlier chapters, we are our own worst enemies. Add our lustful sinful selves and we block or prevent God from moving, or we slow down what He has intended for us all along. So we say, get little, get lower. Become like a child again. God wants us to get back to the basics. Open up. Surrender. Get rid of all the BS we put upon ourselves. Clear it out and repent and let God refill us with the good stuff. He wants us to get back to being open and willing, trusting, forgiving and loving like when we were born. As a child.

Now don't get me wrong. God, Jesus wants us to mature in our actions and beliefs. Our behaviors and values. But He also wants us, and we need to remain like little kids in our trust and dependence towards Him. Let me repeat this. Trust and dependence towards Him.

"As obedient children, do not conform to the evil desires you had when you lived in ignorance" (1 Peter 1:14).

"You, dear children are from God and have overcome them, because the one who is in you is greater than the one who is in the world" (1 John 4:4).

"My dear children, for whom I am again in the pains of childbirth until Christ is formed in you" (Galatians 4:15).

"Yet to all who did receive Him to those who believed His name, He gave the rights to become children of God" (John 1:12).

So we clearly see now that our heavenly father wants us first and foremost to know we are His precious children. When we present ourselves we should lean on Him, humbly seek His care for us, showing faith in Him, then He will in turn work His works in us. Simply put, as we grow if we don't get the proper love or care this causes issues, not the least of which is fear. From the very beginning, from our birth we're never a part of the plan, the real plan. God's plan for us. So now we must go to God, like at the beginning as children, little children. Childish or we will never walk the right walk that God desires. We have to and we must humbly lean on His power and strength, and always and in everything ask for His guidance and help. Remember that we can do nothing that He has called and wants us to do, and what we are all seeking without His help. We must come openly and honestly in total submissive surrender. How childish? Exactly.

Change, Change, Change

I talked previously about man-made laws and how they're failing. When we attempt to make the necessary changes we feel are needed we end up with more laws to force fix all our problems. Will this work? Has this helped any society for the long haul? Has any society survived with this thinking? Well, let's take a little closer look.

Man in the Mirror

"I'm starting with the man in the mirror.
I'm asking him to change his ways.
And no message could've been any clearer
If you wanna make the world a better place
Take a look at yourself and then make a change."

Excerpt from song <u>Man in the Mirror</u>
Written by Glen Ballard and Siedah Garrett
Performed by Michael Jackson

Change. A hard description and honest look at our society. Today you know we have grown up learning to live in a society or should I say "our" society that has always been up until now the richest or one of the wealthiest in the world. But not anymore. We're declining. Let me go on. Let's talk about this. Let's look at the holes, the gaps in this so-called richest society in the world. The gaps I'm talking about between our rich and our poor. Unbelieveable, right? From the beginning of this book I've written about priorities and how our moral values are becoming more and more screwed up. Just look at this example of what we as a society pay money for. We do not pay much for the gifted, the blessed or the skillful, do we? We do pay, however, unbelievable vast amounts of money to compensate our executives, lawyers, counselors, advisors, bankers and other such people. How about psychics and dream readers to help our government and advise our presidents? Wow.

We clearly overpay athletes of all kinds. How many of them drive right past the downtowns of our countries, cities and states, right past the homeless people, the addicts and the prostitutes on their way to the arenas or stadiums to play their sport?

We attach lavish rewards and status to celebrate today's idols who are receiving millions from their talents and social media. More often than not, these idols, these stars, send the wrong message to our kids, to all of us actually because, let's face it, it makes more money for them this way. We pay way too much money to Hollywood movie producers. In general, actors and actresses, television or talk-show personalities, regardless of their status, seem to draw more viewers and up the ratings by focusing and exploiting immoral or salacious events rather than positive type issues. And let's not forget to mention the unscrupulous billionaire evangelists who live in mansions and continue to ask for more money for their missions.

On the other hand, we pay too little to the areas that could and will benefit us. Like scholars, and one of the most critical areas is in our schools. For our children, we need to spend more money and pay more attention to social services, AODA counseling, police and fire personnel, and our health and medical care workers, as well as the emotional and psychological helpers, caregivers and workers. And what about artists and dancers? No one in the entertainment industry, in my opinion, works harder, but in comparison to sports figures they are paid peanuts.

What about alcohol and tobacco use? Every year in the United States, one out of every five people dies from cigarette smoking. This is according to the Centers for Disease Control (CDC). Alcohol-related deaths amount to about 95,000 each year. What about weapons and firearms? They kill more and more people every year and yet people still buy them and these purchases are still legal. Why?

"If you want your children to turn out well, spend twice as much time with them, and half as much money."

Abigail Van Buren

What's Up?

Too many children believe they won't live past 30 to 35 years of age. So why should they care, right? I also understand the number one cause of death in those under age 25 is suicide. Murder and violence has become an everyday occurrence. Kidnappings, assaults and robberies are on the rise and common to a point where we're not even surprised to hear it on the news anymore. Why do we accept all this and yet know deep in our hearts that it is wrong? Why?

Even our justice system exhibits serious signs of defective, inappropriate corrupt behaviors within. This is steadily getting worse. One in five people surveyed, for the most part believe that our justice system is honest. That's less than 20% of people who believe in our justice system, yet we continue to give our government more and more control and power. More man-made laws, more judges with more power. Even probation officers and agents have way too much control and power. That in itself is far too open to human perceptions, errors, confusion and corruption. Why?

Our government dominates the school system now to the point that we don't even come close to the curve of knowledge. As a matter of fact, it's at about a second grade level of understanding in only a 15 year span of time. That's right. Kids learn only as much as a second grade level as kids 15 years past. According to the US Department of Education and the National Institute of Literacy, 32 million people in the United States cannot read. 50% of adults cannot read a book at the eighth grade level. Why?

Our society is a constant victim of urban crimes and there are too many gangs of every race and creed. The government is crowded, confused and corrupt. There are no more true values, morals, boundaries or loyalties. There isn't any real religious influence. Religions have more laws and rules and have now become a man-made deterrent as well. Again, a poorly unsatisfactory educational system. The standard to pass has continued to decrease to a lower degree of accomplishments to complete because the averages keep dropping lower and lower to the point that now anyone can pass or graduate if you just show up and don't carry a weapon or get caught stealing or selling dope. Why? All this within the mix of corrosion and decays of desolate living, unstable family life, broken homes and single parent families trying to do it all on their own.

The widespread disease of drug abuse continues to rise. Suicides are up. Divorces are passed out like penny candies. We have welfare and government induced programs to control us but these are excuses to enable said control based on the lazy values and belief systems with our people. The athletes, the overpaid false idols or those, who intentionally or not, are causing hurt and pain in many more ways then they realize. Our society with the greatest legal system and minds is now sinking on a daily basis. Our society with the most powerful and unbelievable military defense systems in the world were number one. We have the best industries, the best minds, and we impose, or it imposes its beliefs and thoughts to influence its systems of control or otherwise on other foreign lands. Abortion is commonplace and the status of our women grows more worse, day by day. Yes, now I believe you get my point but what you may have missed is this. That this society that I've been trying to give us here a solid honest view of is not new. It's not our society. It's the society back in the Roman empire days. Also, remember the guy they called Caesar? And the pharoahs? Guess what my friend? Guess what happened to that society back then? A system that seems flawless, controlled, pure and right in man's eyes. What happened to it? It fell apart, did it not? It fell apart and died just like that.

So If Nothing Changes, Nothing Changes

"If you keep doing what you did, you keep getting what you got."

Author: Jessie Potter
1981 Milwaukee Sentinel

"The definition of insanity is doing the same thing over and over and expecting different results."

Albert Einstein

God did give us some help. He gave us the Ten Commandments. Simple commonsense rules or instructions so we could avoid all this crap we've been trying to figure out these thousands of years. Why don't we just do it? Deuteronomy Chapter 5 breaks it all down. God said through Moses (to Moses) to us, and He made this covenant to us all.

He said, "I am the LORD your God, who brought you out of Egypt, out of the land of slavery.

You shall have no other gods before me.

You shall not make for yourself in image in the form of anything in heaven above or on the earth beneath or in the waters below. You shall not bow down to them or worship them; for I, the LORD your God, am a jealous God, punishing the children for the sin of the parents to the third and fourth generation of those who hate me, but showing love to a thousand generations of those who love me and keep my commandments.

You shall not misuse the name of the LORD your God, for the LORD will not hold anyone guiltless who misuses His name.

Observe the Sabbath day by keeping it holy, as the LORD your God has commanded you. Six days you shall labor and do all your work, but the seventh day is a Sabbath to the LORD your God. On it you shall not do any work, neither you, nor your son or daughter, nor your male or female servant, nor your ox, your donkey or any of your animals, nor any foreigner residing in your towns, so that your male and female servants may rest, as you do. Remember that you were slaves in Egypt and that the LORD your God brought you out of there with a mighty hand and an outstretched arm. Therefore the LORD your God has commanded you to observe the Sabbath day.

Honor your father and your mother, as the LORD your God has commanded you, so that you may live long and that it may go well with you in the land the LORD your God is giving you.

You shall not murder.

You shall not commit adultery.

You shall not steal.

You shall not give false testimony against your neighbor

These are the commandments the LORD proclaimed in a loud voice to your whole assembly there on the mountain from out of the fire, the cloud and the deep darkness; and He added nothing more. Then He wrote them on two stone tablets and gave them to me."

> *"Hatred never ceases by hatred, but by love only can it be healed."*
> *This is an ancient and an eternal law attributed to Buddha.*

God's law is put in such a way so there can be no mistaking the meaning and the basic fundamental common ingredients for all our human needs to live not only better lives for us as individuals, but also to live together far better as a people or society. This is another example of God's true love for us because when we look at all this, isn't God saying, "Hey you kids, my children. Look I don't expect you to get this all at once and I know you will struggle with a few of them at times but I'll simply write out these tablets for Moses to give to you. When you look at them with a sober and clear level head and in the light of day, your practical intelligence and common sense, along with the conscience I gave you will help you get it all eventually and when you do we'll just keep moving onward and upward."

Simply putting it, no society to date has survived or can pretend to survive with murder and violence, so don't kill. Adultery crushes the family. It is shown too often in movies and on television that it almost is expected as part of life, yet look what this does to society. It's the reason for abuses, for our kids in the streets killing people because of their betrayal issues, abandonment and trust issues. This all starts in the home. That's where we pass it on. So, no adultery. Don't steal. Stealing creates war with each other. We can't have this. Don't steal.

False witness equals trust issues for all. Lying destroys relationships and trusts. Don't lie. Wanting someone else's wife or husband or their property. Lives in jealousy are and will never work out. So God said. Don't covet. And then I'm the Lord your God, no strange Gods before me. Don't take my name in vain. Remember to keep holy God's day and honor our mother and father.

Are these religious rules or laws like so many churches set up throughout society's quest that have kept us stuck? No. So let's be careful. Hear me that we understand legalisms are hurtful to us if we are not careful. I believe that as we continue to grow we sometimes fall a little short depending on the situation. Society's reaction can lead to a whole lot of extra needless and unecessary hurt, pain and suffering. With man's interpretative laws (thousands that man has created), and the laws or rituals of some religions, that becomes a tool of the devil and has stunted our growth for thousands of years.

Don't forget we can't gain one ounce of favor from God by our works alone. So by being able to follow a law, we might believe we somehow are worthy of God's favor, or that we earned it. Big mistake. That won't work.

"For all who rely on the works of the law are under a curse, as it is written: "Cursed is everyone who does not continue to do everything written in the book of the law."

(Galatians 3:10)

The Lord our God has promised that we will be able to do these things within His commandments because He has and will continue to put it in our hearts to do it and the spirit to help us. The motivation as I stated in the first part of this book - the big difference here is internal vs. external motivations. God knows what's on our hearts, not what we think people will approve of or think of us for this or that, but what's in our true selves within our hearts. That internal motivation. He knows if our motives are right or getting better and better that way. Get it? So we don't have to try so hard or get mad, hurt, angry or afraid. We don't have to be full of anxiety, pain or suffering. We just have to want to desire to follow God's simple rules as and only as in our total response to what Jesus has done already for us. It's not to get Him to do something.

Grace. Check This Out.

"For all have sinned, and come short of the glory of God. Being justified freely by his grace through the redemption that is in Christ Jesus. Whom God hath set forth to be a propitiation through faith in His blood. To declare his righteousness for the remission of sins that are past, through the forbearance of God. To declare, I say at this time his righteousness: that he might be just, and the justifier of him which believeth in Jesus."

(Romans 3:23-26)

Faith. Check This Out.

"Where, then, is boasting? It is excluded. Because of what law? The law that requires works? No, because of the law that requires faith. For we maintain that a person is justified by faith apart from the works of the law."

(Romans 3:27-28)

Understand that first we all have to have faith, then we can all do good, but we have to never lose sight of the fact that our works, big or small, do not earn us any particular favor with God. We need to do what we choose to do by pure motives which means we have a desire to give unconditionally and not just to get something in return. Everything that we as a people receive from our loving God is attained by what Jesus did for us and by our faith, and all we have to do is believe.

How childishly simple. Exactly. So in short if we want change, if you want a better self and a better world for all of us, a better life in general, it's simple. God gave us the formula in the beginning. The ten basic rules for us to try and live by and if we do not, not one person who reads this book will be able to disagree that we would be in a much better world.

"Then Jesus said to his disciples, 'Assuredly I say to you that it is easier for a camel to go through the eye of a needle than for a rich man to enter the kingdom of God.' When His disciples heard it, they were greatly astonished, saying, 'Who then can be saved?' But Jesus looked at them and said to them, 'With man this is impossible but with God all things are possible.'"

(Matthew 19:23-26)

Our kids aren't just our kids. They are people's wives and husbands and parents. Nothing on earth will ever make us as happy or sad, as ashamed or as proud, or as completely tired as being our kid's educators. Our kid's parents.

One Nation Under God

One Church

One Love

One God

Is one the lonely number or is one the only number?

A-Z

From the beginning to the end.

A

One Love

One Church

"Love never fails. But where there are prophecies, they will cease; where there are tongues, they will be stilled; where there is knowledge, it will pass away."

(1 Corinthians 13:8)

We have always pondered the quiet silence that comes between the living and the dead. Yet more for their separated and apart are they who live together side by side all life long and yet never heart to heart.

Author: Frank (2009)

As we clearly stated and proved in the first part of I Choose Love, love is the only thing we can take with us from this life on to and through eternity. Love. So it's safe to conclude that love is and always will be the answer. This very important point I've been trying to make clear in this book is that through it all nothing else has withstood the test of time. Nothing else has survived or made it through all man's thinking, judgments and seriously educated plans of action. Nothing has truly worked or has survived except the church.

B

For well over 2000 years, the leaders and all the organized nations, counselors, noblemen, governments, kings, and other leaders have all fallen short. I'm not exactly sure why or how, but for some reason this has started to become so much easier to understand. It has become clearer to see how true it is.

C

Now here's the funniest part of it all. The beginning story of this longest lasting thing, this church. More than 2000 years ago, a man was born not like any other man. This man was not conceived by all the other laws of man. This guy was born of a virgin. This man lived in poverty. He was educated at the Jewish synagogues and at home which was the custom for all Jewish boys. He had no cash flow at all. He also did not have any deep, popular widespread influence with the government, courts or statesmen. He was not worldly and never traveled very far. Actually, He had to walk wherever He went from the little town where He lived. This man never wrote a book but His life has been the true inspiration of more books written to date than any other man. He sang hymns to his Father as mentioned in Romans 15:9 and His life has been the means and topic of more songs than any other man ever.

D

He never went to college yet all the teachers, scholars, educational institutions and schools of our world all put together wish they had more students like Him. This man never joined the army, navy, air force, or marines. He never marshalled nor recruited a soldier. He never used a weapon or fired a gun. Yet no general or other leader to date has had more people, good or bad, surrender their lives to this guy without a punch thrown, a weapon drawn or a gun ever being fired.

E

He was not a doctor. He had no medical education, yet he did heal the sick, the blind, the crippled, the deaf, the lepers and more. He healed them all.

He was not a psychiatrist or psychologist. He had no degrees in social service or counseling, yet this man has healed more broken hearts and comforted more lost and troubled souls than all the doctors of this world. Even today all the world pauses at least once a week to praise and worship this guy. This man is the one who started this one church I'm speaking of. This man and this one church has lasted and spread from His time and His generation to ours. It is without a doubt still alive and very well today.

F

His enemies could not defeat Him. Even the grave could not keep Him or hold Him. Even the grave.

Jesus Christ is clearly much more than a man who started a church. All the evidence is overwhelming. This Jesus and this church, with the love that it will always stand for will transcend the ordinary changes and all the pain and suffering of mind and body. Throughout all of history, the church continues to go far beyond that which we look for and need.

All the other societies that have come and gone like the fall of Rome in the fourth century shows that one thing is starting to make all the sense in the world. Understand?

One God. One church. One love. Amen.

How childishly simple. Exactly.

G

"Come and hear, all you who fear God; let me tell you what he has done for me. I cried out to him with my mouth; his praise was on my tongue. If I had cherished sin in my heart, the Lord would not have listened, but God has surely listened and has heard my prayer. Praise be to God, who has not rejected my prayer or withheld his love from me."

(Psalm 66:16-20)

God knows your heart.

Recovery is not here just to make you feel better or live a happier life. It is here to destroy your idols and make you God's child.

One day I was high as hell on cocaine. My associates (at the time) and I were in a downtown area doing our usual routine of clubbing, wine and women. Cocaine, champagne, and sexy women was the model so to speak. Then across the street from the jailhouse, we saw a line of about a thousand people. Men and women of all races. Where's the concert? Who's playing? What's going on? How come we didn't hear about this?

One of the guys in the line was around my age so I asked him what was going on. He told me and my friends that this line was for just a few of the people who were in trouble breaking the laws to support their drug habits. He said they were mainly cocaine addicts and they have to come to this place all the time to prove they are staying clean and sober. One of my friends, who overhead the conversation said, "all of them?" The guy in the line said "Yes, and there are so many more, all ages, all races."

Sin and drugs don't discriminate

I discovered this much later. That man's laws, although neeeded at times, was missing something.

As we see when we read what all the psalmists are talking and singing about. You see the long line of ongoing screw-ups should have been a sign for me and all of us using drugs and living a life of sin. When the psalmists discovered how to live a better purer life they all seem to be saying that the key is to obey God's teachings, His laws.

"I have hidden our word in my heart that I might not sin against you. Praise be to you Lord; teach me your decrees."

(Psalm 119:11-12)

In the light of God's word we clearly can see our sins.
But we will also see God's love in Christ. By His grace.

H

You see I threw that in here because I had to begin, at least in my heart to want to be clean and live a more pleasing good life to God and others. The list of my sinful activities and thoughts are many during this time of my addictive lifestyle. If I'd continue to dwell on the past or think about this it is depressing and frustrating. I know that you also become frustrated, worried and even disappointed when life isn't working the way we think it should. Thus, the pain and suffering. It's clearer to me now that it just seems that anything I did or tried apart from God didn't work and now it's crystal clear it never will. For any of us. Not for any substantial period of time or for any true lasting value. In short, to fulfill His plan for the world, the world He created, and make way to a salvation known to all we need to follow His instructions.

"Life's a beautiful song that God is teaching us all to play together."

Frank

Let me continue. A-Z, right? We see a very simple reason that people of all races, gender and age have to doubt the existence of a creator, of a God. And love and the church I've been talking about. It's because so many have endured much pain and suffering. Am I right? There has been so much cruelty and evil in the world and that has brought a lot of suffering to innocent people and to innocent victims.

So again the question is asked, "If there is a God why does He allow or permit cruelty and evil?"

Let's start at the very beginning and see if we can't get to Z, okay?

I

The Beginning

We can perhaps find our answer in the opening chapters of Genesis. You see in the beginning it describes the creation of our world and everything in it is without any suffering. The first man and woman, Adam and Eve, were put by God in no less than a tremendous tropical paradise-like setting in a garden-like atmosphere. This was their home and it was called Eden and they were to do challenging yet pleasant work. They were given instructions by God to work the earth, cultivate the grounds and to grow stuff and take care of it. They were also given the management to oversee the waters and the seas and the fish. They were to oversee the birds in the sky, all of them, and even the animals and living creatures moving within the earth itself.

"God blessed them and said to them, 'be fruitful and increase in number, fill the earth and subdue it. Rule over the fish in the sea and the birds in the sky and over every living creature that moves on the ground.'"

(Genesis 1:28)

"The Lord God took the man and put him in the Garden of Eden to work it and take care of it."

(Genesis 2:15)

J

It is important to realize and know that Adam and Eve were created with not only perfect minds but also perfect bodies. They were without any defects whatsoever. None. Knowing this, was it in God's plan for us to have pain and suffering? Let's continue from the beginning to the end.

So in being of perfect mind and body and in charge of all life and food, there was absolutely no reason whatsoever for them to experience pain or suffering. There was no possible reason to suffer from disease, addictions, sickness, old age, or even death for that matter. On the contrary, Adam and Eve had a golden opportunity for a glorious endless existence and future in an earthly paradise.

K

"Listen, you heavens, and I will speak; hear you earth, the words of my mouth. Let my teachings fall like rain and my words descend like dew, like showers of new grass, like abundant rain on tender plants. I will proclaim the name of the Lord, oh praise the greatness of our God. He is the Rock, His words are perfect, and all His ways are just; a faithful God who does no wrong, upright and just is He."

(Deuteronomy 32:1-4)

This first couple, Adam and Eve, were given permission to have children and to have them abundantly, as illustrated in Genesis 1:28, "To be fruitful, become many and fill the earth."

So as they bore children the human population would increase and also be a family unit. And this human family would eventually spread out and continue to increase and expand across all of the earthly paradise in a perfect unity of one family, one love and one God. All in perfect health, no pain, no suffering. A true paradise on earth.

L

God's Rules. God's Laws.

Understanding Genesis as we do, and knowing what we know about Adam and Eve, we see that to continue in peace and harmony we had to be willing to accept and adhere to the Creator's rules and his basic reasonable philosophies. A Creator would and should plan or dictate our affairs so they will stand the test of time and work. Now here's an important part. Why did our God have a few rules? Because it is necessary. First, the creator, maker or inventor of anything has a right to establish and maintain control over that which he has created, made or invented. This is a basic principle of business management. We all had to accept the simple and crucial fact that we were never designed with the ability to control, govern, organize or live in peace and harmony successfully apart from our Creator. The Bible has always been correct as stated in Jeremiah 10:23.

> *"Lord, I know that people's lives are not their own; it is not for them to direct their steps."*
>
> (Jeremiah 10:23)

So we see again God's plan, His original plan was clear and so simple. Simply childish you would say. Exactly. As long as we mere humans lived within the very basic rules or guidelines set up by God at the very beginning, life as we now know it would have been happy, joyful, successful without pain, hurt or suffering. A paradise on earth for all.

M

Free at Last?

Now as we go on, we the people, were also created to have a free will. We were not to be as computers or robots. We were not to do things compulsively or instinctively either. In fact, the freedom given to us by God was to be used in an intelligent and responsible manner and was to be used within the boundaries of God's law. Laws that clearly work for our common good without question. God knew that without law and order to help us in all encounters, we would fall short and stumble and eventually end up in destruction or in a state of anarchy. And our lives would be negatively affected perhaps forever.

Therefore, as we know by our experiences, these freedoms are nice but like anything else too much of anything is not good for us. If you give a young person too much freedom he may play in the streets and go to all the wrong places. We've been looking at all the negative drama we created for ourselves throughout our lives when we were using our own power and free will without using God, our Creator's directions. As with us today that was the reason all our problems had started. Adam and Eve, the first humans, chose to misuse their gifts from God. Like the gift of this freedom, they made the wrong choice. They got over-confident within themselves to go for more freedom and be independent under their own power and strength. They believed they could make the determination as to what was good or bad, and what was right and wrong. In fact, they were acting like God's themselves.

"You will not certainly die," the serpent said to the woman. "For God knows that when you eat from it your eyes will be opened, and you will be like God, knowing good and evil."

(Genesis 3:4-5)

We see here that Adam and Eve turned away or pulled away from God willfully. They chose this course of freedom from their maker. God, being God, let them be free or on their own for a while. "The Lord is with you when you are with Him. If you seek Him He will be found by you, but if you forsake Him, He will forsake you" (2 Chronicles 15:2).

We see that without God and His grace, protection and power, a gradual coming apart, or separation was sure to happen and it did. A breakdown of mind and body started, then in time Adam and Eve grew old and died.

N

Life is not fair. All the time it seems to be the wrong ones getting sick, and the wrong people who get robbed or hurt in crimes. The wrong people seem to get killed in the street or in wars, even by accident. Many of us see this stuff and say to others that there is no God. The world is nothing but unfair and corrupt. It's evil, full of mayhem. I believe we all pondered this question at one time or another with our lives. As a matter of fact I'm sure of it. Yet I have to wonder. Because of this last question, if I see (and I do see) all the bad seemingly unreasonable evil or corruption in the world, I have to ask myself where do I get these feelings of anger or outrage? Where do I get this feeling of sympathy and caring? Why does it hurt me so? Why does it seem to bother me more than others? How do I know what is good or bad? Fair and unfair? Doesn't all the instinctive ways we feel or the way we respond come from God? Did He not give us some of Himself? His same caring and feelings of divine anger at the unfairness and injustices in the world. How did we get our conscience? We all have a conscience. How? This alone and in and of itself may be the absolute proof of our God and His true self realities.

"Let your conscience be your guide."

The Bible says this about our conscience, "The spirit of a man is the lamp of the Lord, searching all the inner depths of his heart" (Proverbs 20:27).

O

The Alpha and Omega
I am The Beginning and the Ending
I am the Great I Am

When Adam and Eve self-separated themselves from God, our Creator, they fell away from the perfect selves God had chosen for them. This falling was well before they had their children. However, as a result of their choices, when they did have children, their children were a direct reflection of what the parents had become (which was not good, not perfect and not even completely functional as planned). This is true for children today. Children are a reflection of their parents.

Adam and Eve, the first people, were imperfect because of their choice to separate from our Creator. Going forward, everything from Adam and Eve is what we all inherited. The children they had were born imperfect. This is where the imperfections causing our sickness and disease, our disabilities and even death come from.

So then this imperfection, along with them separating themselves from God and from God's laws opened the doors to all the other human drama we are up against and put ourselves through. All the pain and suffering and so on. And thus began the long stretch of suffering, sorrow, sickness and death.

P

So now where did evil come from? Did human beings create it? The answer is no. God created other very intelligent creatures, not just humans. He already had finished creating several spirit creatures in Heaven just before He created people.

"Where were you when I laid the earth's foundation? Tell me, if you understand. Who marked off its dimensions? Surely you know! Who stretched a measuring line across it? On what were its footings set, or who laid its cornerstone – while the morning stars sang together and all the angels shouted for joy? Who shut up the sea behind doors when it burst forth from the womb, when I made the clouds its garment and wrapped it in thick darkness?"

(Job 38:4-9)

Now get this, these spirit creatures were also free to choose or deny the responsibility of God's direction. His rules. His laws. These spirit creatures were free and one of them chose to do his own thing apart from God. His pride, self desire and greedy ambition got so arrogant and self-centered that it made him think and believe he himself could challenge God and God's authority. So this manipulative spirit dude tempts Adam's wife Eve into believing they could break God's law, but still not die. "Then the serpent said to the woman, "you will not surely die" (Genesis 3:4).

His cunning statements made Eve first and then Adam actually believe they did not need God to be happy together or to have a contented life. He even went so far as to say that lawbreaking would be an improvement for them and would even make them be like God themselves. Well, he did indeed con and convince them to question and challenge God's laws, even questioning God Himself. And for this misrepresentation, he came to be called the devil. Ever since this action which he started he has been an evil influence on all of mankind.

"When tempted, no one should say, 'God is tempting me.' For God cannot be tempted by evil, nor does He tempt anyone, but each person is tempted when they are dragged away by their own evil desire and enticed. Then, after desire has conceived, it gives birth to sin; and sin, when it's full grown, gives birth to death. Don't be deceived, my dear brothers and sisters. Every good and perfect gift is from above, coming down from the Father of the heavenly lights, who does not change like shifting shadows."

(James 1:13-17)

"Jesus, full of the Holy Spirit, left the Jordan and was led by the Spirit into the wilderness, where for forty days He was tempted by the devil. He ate nothing during these days, and at the end of them He was hungry. The devil said to Him, 'If You are the Son of God, tell this stone to become bread.' Jesus answered, 'It is written man shall not live on bread alone.' The devil led Him up to a high place and showed Him in an instant all the kingdoms of the world. And he said to Him, 'I will give you all the authority and splendor, it has been given to me and I can give it to anyone I want to. If you worship me, it will all be Yours.' Jesus answered, it is written: 'Worship the Lord your God and serve Him only.' The devil led Him to Jerusalem and had Him stand on the highest point of the temple, 'If you are the Son of God,' he said, 'Throw Yourself down from here.'"

(Luke 4:1-9)

"Jesus gave them this answer, 'Very truly I tell you, the Son can do nothing by Himself; He can do only what He sees his Father doing, because whatever the Father does the Son also does.'"

(John 5:19)

"The great dragon was hurled down that ancient serpent called the devil, or Satan, who leads the whole world astray. He was hurled to the earth, and his angels with him."

(Revelation 12:9)

Q

The Devil Made Me Do It

So now we have a much clearer understanding and we're only at Q. Here are more questions that can be raised. Like, why didn't God just take the devil and his new followers out of the game then and there? End of story, right? No. God needed and we also needed to get to this understanding and acceptance level. Under our own power could our own independence from God ever give us a fulfilling or lasting peace? Or love or happiness? We've learned the answer to this question is clearly no.

Are the rules of God better for us? Are God's directions better for us? Or would man's laws and direction be better for us? We've learned the answer to this question and the answer is clearly no. God's directions and rules are better for us.

Could mere humans ever successfully run, handle or manage this world without God's help and guidance? We've learned the answer to this question and the answer is clearly no.

Yet what had to happen is we had to learn from trial and error and a whole lot of unwanted pain in order to get to this place. A place where only the passage of time and experiences could teach us and clearly get us to a place of true knowledge and true understanding. God had to wait it out and we in fact needed Him to.

R

For So Long

We now may ask, why God did you take so long or wait so long to get us to this point? Thousands and thousands of years. Why? I'm sure that if He chose to, God could have settled this matter a long time ago. However, this raises some important reasoning questions. Like if God had gotten involved or intervened long ago, then we could have worked it out within ourselves. We would argue that if given enough time we would have and could have figured it all out. Right? Isn't that how we are? Isn't that how we've been through history? So an accusation would have been made that we were not given enough of a chance to develop a working government or enough time to get to the necessary technologies to deliver us to a joyful and peaceful life that included prosperity for all. So of course God knew this ahead of time like He knows all and gave us the time. He allowed it.

S

Throughout history, there have been many experts in various industries like social services, banking, government and technology who have tried to take charge of our lives. These industries have provided jobs and the ability to go to the moon, enhance the capabilities of the internet and other far-reaching activities. But to what end? Has any of this given us what we long for with the words in our hearts? Has any of this given us the kind of lives that are a true and real blessing to everyone? Our race, our total human family? One nation under God. One Love. One Church. Has it?

T

If we're even a little bit honest, it would be safe to say that the answer to the important question for the hope and survival of mankind is no. We do not have the world we desired. We're way off and headed in the wrong direction. Nothing that the people have tried has even gotten close to true fulfillment, peace, joy, love or happiness. Instead I think we're ending up on shaky ground more often. Crimes are worse or as bad as ever. The family structure is not as strong as it should be. The issues of the homeless and the hungry continue. Our existence has even been jeopardized with our brilliant scientists making and creating nuclear weapons of absolute, almost total destruction. Power that can destroy most, if not all of the human race. Really? Why?

Therefore, despite all the years of human effort and experiences to build on; despite incredible researchers and the progress we have made in so many areas, it is becoming clearer that we're not only unsuccessful but we most likely will not and cannot find success on our own.

U

I also said it seems, at times, to be going in the wrong direction. Let's not just look at the failing conditions of man and woman, let's look briefly at the beautiful planet God gave us which we are messing up. Why? Even God's gift to us, our earth, has been negatively dealt with or cared for by us. Our greed and our lack of vision, our neglect for what's good and right, has slowly begun to destroy beautiful healthy lands into desert land. We strip the forests that protect us and our land. We use far too many chemicals and tons of waste products have polluted all our land, our sea and air. I'll keep this short here. You get what I mean, don't you?

"Because the creation itself also will be delivered from the bondage of corruption into the glorious liberty of the children of God. For we know that the whole creation groans and labors with birth pangs together until now."

(Romans 8:21-22)

"Remember to never begin to not begin to use any of this as excuses or to be less determined like I did."

Author Unknown

"And whatsoever you do, do it heartily, as to the Lord and not to men."

(Colossians 3:23)

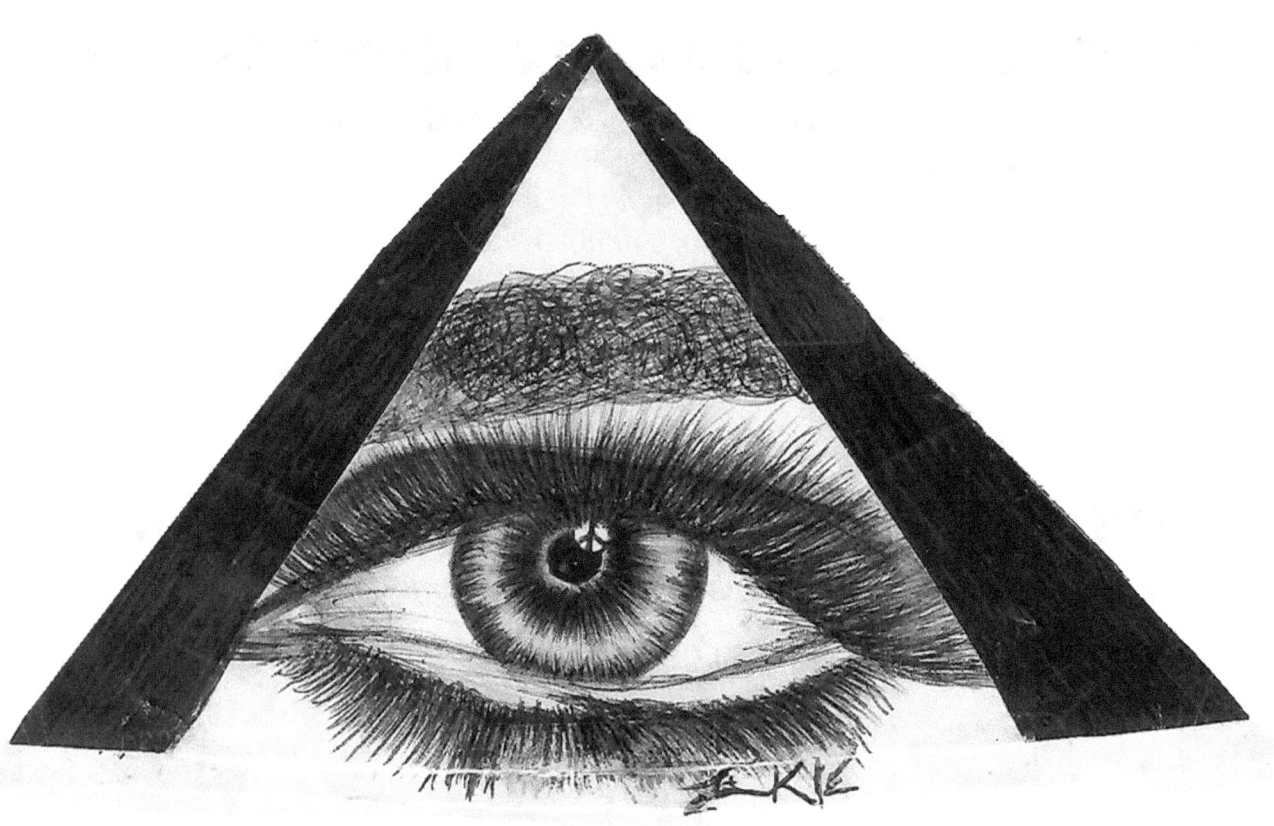

V

Prove It

The Facts Are the Facts

So what does all this mean? What is it all about? What have all these many events in our times proven without a doubt? It's crystal clear that us trying to rule the earth without God's help won't and cannot work. Clearly it has been established that any attempt to be successful in the functioning and simple management of all our earthly affairs is useless and won't work when we're away from our God. History has proven what it says in the Bible.

"All this I saw, as I applied my mind to everything done under the sun. There is a time when a man lords it over others to his own hurt. Then too, I saw the wicked buried in those who used to come and go from the holy place and receive praise in the city where they did this. This too is meaningless."

(Ecclesiastes 8:9-10)

How have all our human attempts worked out when we compare them to the grace and absolute precision we see in our world as it is directed by God's laws? It's been proven and is clear that we need the same guidance and laws. Those of our God. So it truly has been demonstrated over and over again that we have an absolute need for God's help and direction.

W

Perceptions of Time

Also, we now have a little better perspective on time which we talked about earlier. How we see time compared to how others see time. And how God sees the same amount of time. God has proven His point and has also established that we can't even begin and should not complain or challenge Him when it comes to our future. We have no leg to stand on because He proved otherwise. Right? The issue should now be settled. We, the people cannot bring anything we desire or positive things always wanted if and when we try it without God. Period.

So in the future guess what? Pay attention here now. In the future it is no longer necessary to allow years to pass to try to again prove God's point that has already been proven. His points are very clear. Everything that needed to be proven has been proven. The Bible says this:

"Whatever you plot against the Lord, He will bring it to complete destruction. Oppression will not rise up a second time."

(Nahum 1:9)

X

The Solution

You don't need a solution if there isn't a problem. Just like we need a problem to have to find a solution.

I know at times reading and getting to the truth hurts a lot and yes, there has been so much pain and suffering. I know. God knows I know, and yes, we found good and true explanations as to the reasoning behind said pain and suffering. Now here's a good part.

The Bible does show us what's next and when, and even how God will use His power to remove all the suffering and also remove all those who cause it.

Proverbs 2:21 says, "For the upright will live in the land and the blameless will remain in it."

"The nations were angry and your wrath has come. The time has come for judging the dead, and for rewarding your servants the prophets, and a people who revere your name, both great and small, and for destroying those who destroy the earth."

(Revelation 11:18)

> *"The God of peace will soon crush Satan's feet. The grace of our Lord Jesus be with you."*
>
> *(Romans 16:20)*

I think, in fact I now know that it's a safe bet that God will not allow this to go on and on forever. Romans 12:2 says, "And be not conformed to this world, but be yet transformed by the renewing of your mind that ye may prove what is that good, and acceptable, and perfect, will of God."

It's safe to say that when God does put all this back completely in order and He will, be sure of that, He will not let anything or anyone stop Him. They won't even be able to try. He gave us all the time we needed and wanted and still we failed.

Y

Temporary Pain Equals Long Term Benefits

Let me share a quick story about my sister Candie. You may remember in the first part of this book, I had talked a little about how she handled her polio. How she always remained positive and determined. She showed and taught us all great lessons in love and acceptance. She raised a big family while going through life with polio and a bad leg. What a wonderful example of how we are to be. Thank you Candie.

We were at a pet shop one day to find a puppy. We did find one and if I remember correctly we called her Jessica. At the store, we sat in front of a big cage full of dogs, big and small, and all different colors and breeds. Lots of dogs. I believe it was the manager of the store who saw my sister and me sitting there, looking at the dogs with big eyes, and he asked if we wanted to see the dogs up close. "Yes, could we?" He agreed and all the dogs came tumbling out toward us ready to play. Except for one little puppy at the back of the cage. We then noticed that the dog in the back could not walk very well, as one of its legs was messed up pretty badly. Candie asked the manager how much the dogs cost. The manager said, "Well, kids I ususally get more, but for you $27.00." Candie told him we only had $14 and asked if we could work for the rest. The manager agreed and asked which dog we wanted.

Candie said she wanted that one and she pointed to the dog in the back of the cage. The manager said, "No, no dear, you don't want that one. That one is damaged. Pick out another one." Candie insisted that was the dog we wanted. The manager then said to us kids that we could have that one for nothing. He would give it to us. But Candie said, "No, no, he's worth every bit as much as the others." As my sister and I got up and walked around the counter to pay, the manager was able to see that Candie was wearing a brace and had a bad limp. The manager asked my sister, "Why do you want that one?" My sister replied, "I understand him. He needs me."

While the suffering over the years has been painful for those of us victimized by it, it has also served a good and lasting purpose. Let's look at it in its true reality and clearly see that it is kind of like going into a hospital and getting an operation to correct a major issue or problem. In the long run, the benefits truly outweigh the temporary pain. Knowing this, know also that God has a purpose for all of us and for this earth. He will indeed fix it all.

> *"See, I will create new heavens and a new earth. The former things will not be remembered, nor will they come to mind."*
>
> *(Isaiah 65:17)*

So we see all suffering will be removed and taken from our memories. Then the joy will overwhelm or push away all the bad memories for God "will wipe every tear from their eyes. There will be no more death or mourning or crying or pain, for the old order of things has passed away. He who was seated at the throne said, "I am making everything new, then He said, 'Write this down, for these words are trustworthy and true'" (Revelation 21:4-5).

Z

Get Childish

Surrender all that is sin, that is of bitterness, that is resentful or hopeless in your lives. Surrender everything that is of other idols, of magic, witchcraft, superstitions or any act of darkness from our past.

Surrender all of our past sins and those who sinned against us all.

The Father, the Son and the Holy Spirit knows and sees the situations we are in and sees that we are powerless to change without them. We need to give them all our mistakes and all our BS, all our circumstances and any and all things that block our hope. Give this to them. We must get like children and let the Father, Son and Holy Spirit break down all the walls we built and break all the chains we bound ourselves up in. Let them loosen all the ties that keep us bound up.

There's nothing they will not do so we all may grow. There's nothing they cannot do so we all may grow. All it takes is our willingness. Our willingness. Our willingness and their power. Their power. Their power.

Without the Father, the Son and the Holy Spirit and us together, there can be no growth within us. Together we will grow. Alone we cannot!

Let's not forget here that all I've been talking about; all this process is just that, a process. From a sinful life to a life of holiness. And there's no way for us to do it but by God's roads of grace.

"And I heard a loud voice from the throne saying, 'Look. God's dwelling place is now among the people and He will dwell with them. They will be His people, and God Himself will be with them and be their God.'"

(Revelation 21:3)

Jesus also speaks of the "coming re-creation" in Matthew 19.

The past victims of suffering and death will learn that God does care, because all then will see God's recreating of those who are already dead in the graves. John 5:28 states, "Do not be amazed at this, for a time is coming when all who are in their graves will hear His voice."

In this way the dead will also be given the opportunity to submit to God's righteous rule and gain the privilege of living forever. Jesus said in Luke 23:34, "Truly I say to you, today you will be with me in paradise."

"The wolf will live with the lamb, the leopard will lie down with the goat; the calf and the lion and the yearling together; and a little child will lead them. The cow will feed with the bear, their young will lie down together, and the lion will eat straw like the ox. The infant will play near the cobra's den, and the young child will put its hands into the viper's nest. They will neither harm nor destroy on all my holy mountain; for the earth will be filled with the knowledge of the Lord as the waters cover the sea."

(Isaiah 11:6-9)

And as it says in Romans 8:21, "That the creation itself will be liberated from the bondage to decay and brought into the freedom and glory of the children of God."

In time the earth will become a paradise inhabited by perfect people, free from sickness and sorrow and death. Suffering will be forever a thing of the past. All aspects of God's earthly creation will come into complete harmony with His purpose. The end or the beginning?

In or out? It's simply a choice. How childish. Exactly.

Final Thoughts

When you're doing what you love to do you don't need any motivation.

So now, what's up? Are you maybe going to pray a little more than you used to? Are you going to allow God to love you more and are you going to love Him back? If you are, then all I can say is watch out my friend because you're going to take a wonderful trip in the here and now on earth and on through to Heaven. So fasten your seatbelts. Really. I mean it. We each must continue to prepare ourselves, take our stand and make some positive changes. For ourselves, for history and for today, tomorrow and through all eternity. This is big. Huge. Just smile now because if we all begin to practice what we have been talking about within this book, we are without a doubt going to find God's compassion. We're going to find God's power. We're going to learn and find His plan for us and we're going to learn and find His love.

"Blessed is the man who perseveres under trial because when he has stood his test, he will receive the crown of life that God has promised those who love Him" (James 1:12).

Let's remember that we are the biggest roadblocks and obstacles that get in our loving God's way, while He's slowly, but surely molding us into what He wants us to be. In Alcoholics Anonymous (AA), Narcotics Anonymous (NA) or even Cocaine Anonymous (CA) they teach us a very important lesson and that is one should take a moral inventory on a daily basis and when we're wrong promptly admit it. This is as important in our recovery programs as it is in all of our lives as sinful humans that will continue to make mistakes. These mistakes become our very own stumbling blocks for our advancement and growth. This is no secret and is true. It's also true that we all are very guilty of putting roadblocks and obstacles in the way of others as well by our fault finding, judgmental attitudes and ways. This is a very strong tool that the devil uses so let's do our best to stop it okay? I also came to understand a long time ago that it is easier to pick on others because it takes the focus off of you and therefore, we don't have to put the work into ourselves that's required in order to make the necessary positive changes we need to make, many of which are usually very hard to do. Also, according to an old Native American saying, "When we point a finger at someone else if we look real close three fingers are pointing back at you." Go ahead, try it!

So please understand this. Avoiding the faults that need to be corrected within ourselves and within our own lives not only slows down your own growth but also slows down and prevents some, if not most, of God's effectiveness through the lives of those around you. Consider this important fact: God's effectiveness in or through us is either enhanced, diminished or hindered by how we think, feel, behave or by the way we live.

"Therefore, let us stop passing judgment on one another. Instead make up your mind not to put any stumbling blocks or obstacles in your brother's way" (Romans 14:13).

Remember the pipeline example earlier in this book? If the pipe is clean the flow is better, stronger and easier through it. Remember, we're in control of what we allow to block the flow by our bad or good choices. Did I just make us a little more responsible there? Yes I did, didn't I? We must always keep in mind that our Number One priority is love and that anything, and I mean anything, that gets in our way and gets into our God's way is without a doubt useless and dispensable, even the important things some of society today deems appropriate. If we are to practice this new lifestyle, this walk of life, we have to be true and useful for God. We can never lose sight of the fact that it's all God to begin with. His love, His everything. So, let's start all of us here by taking our little "obstacle" moral inventories on a daily basis and when we are wrong promptly admit it and ask for forgiveness. Even when and if the stumbling blocks or obstacles appear to be legitimate in the eyes of society, by using our newfound knowledge and wisdom given to us by God, we should not be fooled out of seeing things as they really are.

Sin is clearly obstructive to us and to others. Things like gossip, bitterness, greed, abuse, boasting, slander, anger, revenge and selfishness all close up the heart to the all-important messages and plans of our loving God. If we keep our hearts closed up in sin, He can't flow through us. A good start here for me and for us all is to get rid of those things listed above and replace them with these instead: humility instead of boasting; gentleness instead of anger and abuses; patience instead of bitterness. A constant unity among us all to walk together as one in a bond of peace in a bond of love. Can we? Yes, we can! Let's start today, right now.

Flashback Recaps

- ✓ Nobody can force you to change your beliefs or what's on and in your heart on the inside. God sees and knows the hearts of all of us.
- ✓ Love is the only thing we take from this life on earth to Heaven and into eternity with us. All else will vanish away.
- ✓ All the scholars and experts commonly refer to love in all their written works.
- ✓ Jesus said the most important commandment is to love your God with all your heart, and love your neighbors as yourself.
- ✓ God also said we must all abide in faith, hope and love, but the greatest of these is love.
- ✓ Love is in fact the strongest emotion and impact on earth as it will leave a legacy behind as well.
- ✓ We are the biggest obstacle of this all important part of our lives. But we can choose to change and fix this.
- ✓ God has been from the beginning and still is today, waiting for all of us to walk in His planned love for us and when we finally do – look out!
- ✓ It should be clear by now that love is the key. Love is the answer.

What's life all about? What's the meaning of life?

It's all about LOVE.

Let's remember to always check our motives. As stated earlier in this book, we should not only do an inventory but examine and evaluate ourselves to see whether our motives are pure. Don't forget God always knows what's truly on the heart. Remember we also talked about external vs. internal motivation. External is for outside sources and usually for all the wrong reasons. Internal is the good stuff (of the heart) and usually pure and true. And, also let's not forget why taking an inventory is so important. With the world the way it is today, sometimes we do things because it's the normal thing to do or what the government or the powerful people say is the right thing to do. And sometimes we don't even know our motives because we don't search our own hearts to discover them. Make taking inventory a habit and practice it every day. Sometimes it is easy to become accustomed to doing things (good or bad) without ever realizing why. I've done this plenty of times. So again, let's be aware. It's not actually what we do that will impress God, but it is why we do it. It's easy and people may become impressed with what we do, but God is not. God knows our hearts and if our motives are pure.

Do not allow the different religions and denominations to confuse the real truth. God hates sin but loves the sinner. He hates stubbornness and rebellion, but still loves the person who is stubborn and rebellious. He has not told us we have to approve of everyone's beliefs, thoughts, choices or actions, but He has told us to love everyone. Today there are so very many denominations and independent cults and churches and the devil loves it because he can use it to cause friction, confusion and separation. Yet know and remember and let's all believe this. There is only one Bible. It is clear that God has the same message to say to all people and one plan for our conduct and relationship with Him.

One Bible ⟶ One message to all people ⟶ One plan = One Love.

"The Lord does not look at the things man looks at. Man looks at the outward appearance, but the Lord looks at the heart."

(1 Samuel 16:7)

Beware of colors. The devil uses prejudice as another of its greatest tools to block the progress of God, as well as our own progress. Some Jews still today spend their time hating all Germans because of Adolf Hitler. There are Americans who still hate the Japanese because of WWII and the bombing of Pearl Harbor. There are African Americans who still hate white people because of slavery. We cannot go back and undo the past. We cannot pay people back for what was done, good or bad. That is God's work to handle. Let's all forget what's behind us and press on to this new, bright loving future ahead for all of us in our new walk of love.

Are you with me here? How sad I was and have been all my life up until just recently, holding onto resentments. Spending all that time in this bitter hate because I was abused, or hating some family members for abandoning me or rejecting me, or hating all church people because some had beaten me or even betrayed me. Yes, all this is true but this life is too short and we won't get anywhere positive if we spend it hating.

Remember (especially as we all start to practice this new life) our enemy is Satan, who wants to destroy us all. We can't waste our time and strength fighting each other (which is what he wants); let's rather walk in love and we will defeat him guaranteed.

Conclusions

"If I speak in the tongues of men and of angels, but have not love, I am only a resounding gong or a clanging cymbal. If I have the gift of prophecy and can fathom all mysteries and all knowledge, and if I have a faith that can move mountains, but have not love, I am nothing. If I give all I possess to the poor and surrender my body to the flames, but have not love, I gain nothing.

Love is patient, love is kind. It does not envy, it does not boast, it is not proud. It is not rude, it is not self-seeking, it is not easily angered, it keeps no record of wrongs. Love does not delight in evil but rejoices with the truth. It always protects, always trusts, always hopes, and always perseveres.

Love never fails. But where there are prophecies, they will cease; where there are tongues, they will be stilled; where there is knowledge, it will pass away. For we know in part and we prophesy in part, but when perfection comes, the imperfect disappears. When I was a child, I talked like a child. I thought like a child. I reasoned like a child. When I became a man, I put childish ways behind me. Now I see but a poor reflection as in a mirror, then we shall see face to face. Now I know in part, then I shall know fully, even as I am fully known.

And now these three remains: faith, hope and love. But the greatest of these is love" (1 Corinthians 13:1-13).

As we near the end of this book, it should be clear to you by now that love is the most important and greatest gift in our lives and in life. Period. It is the true meaning of life. It is the reason we are here and so walking in love and living in love should be, and has to be our Number One priority and our Number One focus. God is, always was, and always will be love, and in turn He wants us to love one another too. We learned that we can only love one another by getting and giving God's love. How do we do it? By finally beginning to understand that He loves us, and understand and accept His love. When we truly do, we will in fact begin a "love walk" that not only allows us, but the world around us, one person at a time, one day at a time, to live in a far better way, a new way. A new way of thinking. A new way of speaking. A new way of believing, feeling and acting, and a new way of responding. One person at a time, one day at a time.

Our new lifestyle of love can and will be expressed in many ways as we all begin this new practice. But one thing will always be true. Love gives. Also we know now that love, whether geared toward fellow believers or not, is not the impulsive thing we may have thought it once was based on feelings. And we have learned that love does not always fit the norm or natural inclinations of life on life's terms and mostly love does not discriminate. It seeks the true pure welfare of all and can do no harm to any, and love always seeks the opportunity to do good to all men and women. Walking in love won't always be natural and there will be times when it isn't easy at all and even impossible. It will take a lot of effort and a lot of sacrifice but we can do it. We can. God made it clear and makes it possible and God does not make mistakes.

As I come to the end of writing this book, my first attempt at writing a book, I'm feeling joyful and excited because this book just might be good enough to get published and it just might, by the grace of God, make a difference to someone. I'm feeling a little overwhelmed and I just wanted to share that with all of you who are reading this. Thank you.

In this book, I have tried to explain as best I could some of the experiences that God has blessed me with and taught me through the years. We have a pretty good starting point here if we begin to practice what is in this book. I also truly believe that if we do begin to practice this within ourselves we will change the world. No doubt! However, I haven't even scratched the surface of what God has in store for us as we start this new journey and walk this new and improved path of love. I can only imagine what's next. Look out world. Here we come. Life is too short so let's start now. Let's not wait any longer now that we have unlocked this mystery and found the answer – the answer to what life is all about. LOVE.

I CHOOSE LOVE.

Epilogue

It is my hope and dream that this book will make a little difference in your life. If it has helped you in any way at all, then please let's pass it on.

Remember life is like a relay race. People before us started the race. We need to learn from them and pass the baton to the next generation. We don't want our kids to make the same mistakes we made, do we? I hope you will share this book with your friends, neighbors and children.

God gave us all free will. We all have choices to make each and every day.

I choose love.

Will you?

Acknowledgements

This book would have not been possible without the inspiration I gained from listening to, or reading about Rick Warren, Joyce Meyer, Dr. James P. Gill, St. Augustine, Thomas Jefferson, Blaise Pascal, Helen Keller, St. Dionysius the Areopagite, Mignon McLaughlin, Albert Einstein, Dr. Charles F. Stanley, Jessie Potter, C.S. Lewis, John Ruskin, Nancy Friday, Pema Chadron, Abigail Van Buren, William Law, Katherine Anne Porter, Edmund Waller, British Clergy Henry Drummond, E.C. McKenzie, Father Andrews, Rose Stokes, Brother Rene Voillaume, and others who I have identified within the pages of this book.

Scripture references are taken from the Holy Bible, New International Version® NIV® Copyright © 1973, 1978, 1984 by International Bible Society®. Used by permission of International Bible Society®. All rights reserved worldwide.

Scripture references were also taken from Amplified Bible Classic Edition (AMPC) and the Hebrew-Greek Key Study Bible, King James Version, Fifth Printing 1988.

Special thanks to Nico 11 Publishing.

And finally, this book would not have happened without the skills and patience exhibited by my girlfriend, Judy, who typed the manuscript from pages and pages of handwritten notes. She edited numerous drafts of my manuscript for punctuation, spelling, and grammar and added class and clarity to my words.

The author felt strongly compelled to write *I Choose Love* so he could share his story and offer his encouragement to others. While this is his first published book, he has written numerous successful outlines, formats, lessons, and modules, as well as articles on Relapse Prevention, Stages of Recovery, Recovery Dynamics, and more.

Get on board.

Love. Love. "Love."

"If we love love, if we love friendship, if we love helpfulness, if we love beauty, if we love health, if we love to create joy, if we love usefulness, if we truly love love and are not self-seekers, the spirit which expresses itself in love (and helpfulness and beauty) will enter into us and abide there and we become what we love."

www.ingramcontent.com/pod-product-compliance
Lightning Source LLC
Chambersburg PA
CBHW081343070526
44578CB00005B/707